GoodFood MAGAZINE

101 CHRISTMAS DISHES
TRIED-AND-TESTED RECIPES

Editor
Angela Nilsen

BOOKS

Contents

Introduction

Anything that can help make the hustle and bustle of cooking at Christmas easier and less stressful is bound to be valuable. Which is why this collection of our favourite festive recipes from *Good Food Magazine* has been carefully selected so that it can cover all your culinary needs.

Whether you are looking for creative ideas for edible gifts to make, quick and inspirational ways to decorate the cake or feed friends when they drop by for a casual drink or more formal supper – they are all here. This little book is packed full of so many new ideas, both traditional and contemporary, from what to serve on Christmas day to impressive make-ahead desserts and clever new twists on baking classics such as mince pies and stollen – you'll find yourself spoilt for choice.

As all the recipes have been carefully tested in the *Good Food* kitchen for their simplicity and flavour, you can rest assured that your Christmas cooking will never be so easy or taste as good.

Angela Nilsen

Angela Nilsen
BBC Good Food Magazine

Conversion tables

NOTES ON THE RECIPES
• Eggs are medium in the UK and Australia (large in America) unless stated otherwise.
• Wash all fresh produce before preparation.
• Recipes contain nutritional analyses for 'sugar', which means the total sugar content including all natural sugars in the ingredients, or 'added sugar' – which is sugar added to the recipe.

OVEN TEMPERATURES

Gas	°C	Fan °C	°F	Oven temp.
¼	110	90	225	Very cool
½	120	100	250	Very cool
1	140	120	275	Cool or slow
2	150	130	300	Cool or slow
3	160	140	325	Warm
4	180	160	350	Moderate
5	190	170	375	Moderately hot
6	200	180	400	Fairly hot
7	220	200	425	Hot
8	230	210	450	Very hot
9	240	220	475	Very hot

APPROXIMATE WEIGHT CONVERSIONS
• All the recipes in this book list both imperial and metric measurements. Conversions are approximate and have been rounded up or down. Follow one set of measurements only; do not mix the two.
• Cup measurements, which are used by cooks in Australia and America, have not been listed here as they vary from ingredient to ingredient. Please use kitchen scales to measure dry/solid ingredients.

SPOON MEASURES

- Spoon measurements are level unless otherwise specified.
- 1 teaspoon = 5ml
- 1 tablespoon = 15ml
- 1 Australian tablespoon = 20ml (cooks in Australia should measure 3 teaspoons where 1 tablespoon is specified in a recipe)

APPROXIMATE LIQUID CONVERSIONS

metric	imperial	AUS	US
50ml	2fl oz	¼ cup	¼ cup
125ml	4fl oz	½ cup	½ cup
175ml	6fl oz	¾ cup	¾ cup
225ml	8fl oz	1 cup	1 cup
300ml	10fl oz/½ pint	½ pint	1¼ cups
450ml	16fl oz	2 cups	2 cups/1 pint
600ml	20fl oz/1 pint	1 pint	2½ cups
1 litre	35fl oz/1¾ pints	1¾ pints	1 quart

A simple, no-hassle mincemeat that makes a delicious
and impressive festive gift.

Blitz n' Blend Mincemeat

50g/2oz blanched almonds
100g/4oz candied peel
1 Bramley apple, peeled, cored and
chopped into large chunks
50g/2oz stem ginger, plus 2 tbsp
syrup from the jar
50g/2oz glacé cherries
50g/2oz ready-to-eat dried
pineapple
225g/8oz each of sultanas, raisins,
currants
140g/5oz shredded suet
225g/8oz light muscovado sugar
a pinch of salt
¼ tsp each powdered ginger,
mixed spice, nutmeg
grated zest and juice 1 orange
150ml/¼pt brandy or dark rum

Takes 20 minutes •
Makes about 1.6kg/3lb 8oz

1 Sterilize the jars. Preheat the oven to
150°C/Gas 2/fan oven 130°C. Use jars with
new rubber seals and spring-clip or screw-
band fastenings, or jam jars with plastic-
coated lids. Wash in hot, soapy water and
rinse. Dry in the oven for 10 minutes.
2 In your food processor, pulse the almonds,
peel, apple, ginger, cherries and pineapple
together until finely chopped (but not mushy)
then tip into a large bowl. In batches, pulse
the sultanas, raisins and currants until just
chopped a little bit, then add to the bowl.
3 Sprinkle the suet and sugar, a pinch of salt
and the spices over all the chopped fruit and
mix well. Pour over the ginger syrup, orange
zest and juice and alcohol, then mix again.
Spoon the mixture into the sterilized jars,
seal and label. Keeps for upto 2 months.

• Per serving (25g) 81 kcalories, protein none,
carbohydrate 14g, fat 2g, saturated fat 1g, fibre none,
added sugar 5g, salt 0.02g

Enjoy these spiced pears with cold meats, cheeses, savoury tarts or pies, topped with a little of their syrup.

Pickled Pears

1 lemon or orange
10 cloves
2 tsp black peppercorns, lightly crushed
1 tsp allspice berries, lightly crushed
5cm/2in piece fresh root ginger, sliced
1 litre/1¾ pints cider or white wine vinegar
2 cinnamon sticks
1kg/2lb 4oz bag caster sugar
2kg/4lb 8oz small pears

Takes 45 minutes, plus a month storing
• Makes enough to fill a 1–1.5 litre kilner jar

1 Pare the zest and squeeze the juice from the lemon or orange. Put in a pan with the cloves, peppercorns, allspice, root ginger, vinegar, cinnamon sticks and sugar. Stir over a gentle heat until the sugar has dissolved.

2 Peel, core and halve the pears, then add to the pan and simmer for 15 minutes, until the pears are tender. Remove the pears with a slotted spoon and put in a colander to drain. Meanwhile, increase the heat under the syrup and boil rapidly for 15 minutes, until the syrup has reduced by about a third and slightly thickened.

3 Pack the fruit into warmed, sterilized jars (see page 10) and pour over the hot syrup to cover. Seal, label and store in a cool, dry place for a month before using.

• Per jar 4553 kcalories, protein 6g, carbohydrate 1203g, fat 2g, saturated fat none, fibre 22g, added sugar 1002g, salt 0.74g

The perfect accompaniment to all festive cold meats, especially cold ham and turkey.

Cranberry, Pineapple and Date Chutney

1kg/2lb 4oz cooking apples
1 medium pineapple (about 500g/1lb 2oz prepared weight)
500g/1lb 2oz onions
350g/12oz cranberries
500g bag stoned dates
250g/9oz raisins
4 garlic cloves, chopped
10cm/4in fresh root ginger, grated
1 tsp chilli flakes
1 tbsp ground cumin
1 tbsp ground coriander
2 tsp ground cinnamon
2 tsp salt
1.5 litres/2¾ pints spiced vinegar
750g/1lb 10oz light muscovado sugar

Takes about 1½ hours •
Makes about 3.2kg/7lb

1 Peel, core and roughly chop the apples and pineapple. Peel and roughly chop the onions. Mix together the apples, pineapple, onions, cranberries, dates, raisins, garlic and ginger.

2 Put the mix of fruit and vegetables in batches through the food processor until finely chopped. Tip into a large wide pan or preserving pan. Add the spices, salt and vinegar and bring to the boil. Simmer for 20 minutes until the apple is pulpy, then add the sugar and stir to dissolve. Bring to the boil, then simmer for about 40–45 minutes, until the chutney is thick and pulpy.

3 Pot into warm, sterilized jars (see page 10). Seal, label and store for at least a month in a cool, dry place.

• Per serving (25g) 46 kcalories, protein none, carbohydrate 1203g, fat none, saturated fat none, fibre 22g, added sugar 1002g, salt 0.74g

A tangy, seasonal dressing, perfect for brightening up
New Year salads after the Christmas excesses.

Christmas Dressing

4 tbsp cranberry sauce
6 tbsp red wine vinegar
2 tsp clear honey
1 tbsp wholegrain mustard
350ml/12 fl oz olive oil
3 sprigs rosemary
2 bay leaves

Takes 5 minutes • Makes about
500ml/18fl oz (easily doubled)

1 Put all the ingredients, except the herbs, into a bowl and whisk lightly to mix. Season to taste.
2 Pour into a sterilized jar or bottle, add the herbs and secure with a lid or cork. Will keep in a cool, dark place for up to 4 weeks.

• Per serving 91 kcalories, protein none, carbohydrate 1g, fat 9.7g, saturated fat 1.4g, fibre none, added sugar 1g, salt 0.02g

Make your Christmas cheeseboard truly festive with these star-shaped, crunchy biscuits.

Thyme-Scented Oatcakes

225g/8oz fine oatmeal (such as pinhead)
2 tbsp fruity olive oil
½ tsp sea salt
3 tbsp fresh thyme leaves or 2 tsp dried
about 8 tbsp boiling water

Takes 30–40 minutes • Makes 20

1 Preheat the oven to 180°C/Gas 4/fan oven 160°C. Tip the oatmeal, oil, salt and 2 tablespoons of the fresh thyme (or 1 teaspoon dried) into a food processor. Whiz to chop and combine. With the motor running, pour in the boiling water. Whiz for 30–45 seconds – the mixture will start to come together and look sticky and thick. Tip in the remaining thyme and pulse to chop roughly.

2 Gather the dough into a ball with your hands. While it's still warm, roll the dough out on a floured surface to a thickness of about 2mm/⅟₁₆in. Cut out using a 6cm/2½in round or a 9cm/3½in star cutter. Place on two greased baking sheets.

3 Bake for 15 minutes or until lightly coloured. Transfer to a wire rack to cool and crisp. They will keep in an airtight tin for 2–3 weeks.

• Per biscuit 48 kcalories, protein 1g, carbohydrate 7g, fat 2g, saturated fat none, fibre 1g, added sugar none, salt 0.13g

Delicious after-dinner treats for
grown-up Christmas celebrations.

Chocolate Tia Maria Nuggets

142ml carton double cream
200g bar dark chocolate, broken up
4 tbsp Tia Maria (or Kahlúa,
Cointreau or Frangelica)
icing sugar and cocoa powder,
to coat

Takes about 20 minutes, plus chilling •
Makes about 30 chocolates

1 Bring the cream to the boil in a small pan.
Remove from the heat and stir in the
chocolate until it has melted. Stir in the
liqueur and pour into a bowl. Cool, then chill
until firm, about 4 hours, or overnight.
2 Sprinkle a sheet of greaseproof paper with
icing sugar and another with cocoa powder.
3 Take a teaspoon and scoop nuggets of
truffle mix out of the bowl and on to either
the paper with cocoa powder or icing sugar.
Use two teaspoons to coat the nuggets then
transfer them to paper sweet cases. Pack in
boxes and chill. Can be stored in the fridge
for up to 2 weeks.

• Per serving 71 kcalories, protein 1g, carbohydrate
7g, fat 4g, saturated fat 3g, fibre none, added sugar
6g, salt 0.04g

Let the children help make these novelty chocolates,
then pack them up in pretty boxes to give as gifts.

Spiced Orange Chocolate Trees

1 orange
225g/8oz milk chocolate, broken
in pieces
¼ tsp ground mixed spice
coloured sugar balls, to decorate

Takes 10–15 minutes, plus 1 hour
chilling • Makes 8 chocolates

1 Using the smallest holes on a grater,
finely grate the zest of the orange.

2 Put the chocolate into a heatproof bowl
and microwave on High (850W) for 1 minute.
Holding the bowl with a cloth, stir the
chocolate. Return it to the microwave on
High for 30 seconds until the chocolate is
just softened. Add the spice and orange zest
and stir to mix.

3 Drop several sugar balls into 8 holes of a
flexible tree-shaped (or other shape such as
star) ice-cube tray. Spoon in the chocolate.
Chill for at least 1 hour, then, with a plate
ready, upturn the ice-cube tray, pressing the
base of each tree to pop out the chocolates.
Can be made ahead and kept in a cool
place for up to a week.

• Per chocolate 131 kcalories, protein 2g,
carbohydrate 14g, fat 8g, saturated fat 5g, fibre none,
sugar 14g, salt 0.06g

Give a taste of Italian Christmas – wrap this nutty delight in clingfilm, overwrap in matt silver paper and tie with gold elasticated string.

Panforte

rice paper, for lining
175g/6oz blanched almonds
50g/2oz walnut halves
100g/4oz shelled hazelnuts
100g/4oz dried figs
175g/6oz candied citron and orange peel
50g/2oz plain flour
25g/1oz cocoa powder
1 tsp ground cinnamon
½ tsp ground coriander
¼ tsp grated nutmeg
175g/6 oz granulated sugar
175g/6oz clear honey
icing sugar, for dusting

Takes 1¼ hours •
Cut into 20–24 wedges

1 Preheat the oven to 180°C/Gas 4/fan oven 160°C. Lightly oil a 20cm/8in sandwich tin and line the base and sides with rice paper, cutting to fit. In a dry frying pan, toast the nuts until lightly tinged. Roughly chop the nuts, finely chop the figs and peel, and mix together. Sift in the flour, cocoa and spices and mix together.

2 Heat the sugar and honey gently in a pan, stirring until the sugar has dissolved. Increase the heat and boil for 2 minutes, until slightly syrupy. Stir well into the dry mix until everything looks moist.

3 Spoon the mixture into the tin and press down. Bake for 45 minutes, then cool for 15 minutes. Turn out on to a wire rack to cool. Sift icing sugar over the top and wrap in clingfilm. Keeps for up to 1 month.

• Per wedge for 20 wedges 221 kcalories, protein 3.5g, carbohydrate 30.2g, fat 10.4g, saturated fat 1g, fibre 2.1g, sugar 25.5g, salt 0.09g

Any unsalted nut will do in this brittle, which makes an ideal homemade gift as it keeps for a few weeks and travels well.

Pistachio Chocolate Brittle

85g/3oz shelled unsalted pistachio nuts
350g/12oz dark chocolate, roughly broken
175g/6oz milk chocolate, roughly chopped
175g/6oz white chocolate, roughly chopped
rice paper, for lining
cocoa powder, to dust (optional)

Takes 20 minutes • Makes about 800g/1lb 12oz

1 Cover the pistachios with water and leave for 2 minutes. Rub between sheets of paper to remove skins. Melt 100g/4oz of the dark chocolate in a bowl set over a pan of gently simmering water (or microwave on High for about 2 minutes). Remove from the heat.
2 Line the base and part way up the sides of a 20cm/8in square tin with rice paper. Spread the melted chocolate, scatter with chopped milk and white chocolates and pistachios. Melt remaining dark chocolate and pour over. Leave to set.
3 Best made 1–2 days ahead and kept in a cool place, or chill. If the surface develops a white bloom, just dust it lightly with cocoa powder. Before wrapping, break into jagged pieces using the tip of a knife.

• Per 25g (2oz) 130 kcalories, protein 1.9g, carbohydrate 13.6g, fat 7.9g, saturated 3.9g, fibre 0.3g, sugar 13.4g, salt 0.03g

Get ahead with this classic, basic Christmas cake. Make it several months in advance, and it will keep until you are ready to decorate.

Classic Christmas Cake

225g/8oz butter, softened to room temperature
225g/8oz dark muscovado sugar
225g/8oz plain flour
4 eggs, beaten
50g/2oz ground almonds
100ml/3½fl oz sweet or dry sherry
85g/3oz candied peel, roughly chopped
85g/3oz glacé cherries, roughly chopped
250g/9oz raisins
250g/9oz currants
100g/14oz pecans, in pieces
finely grated zest 1 lemon
1½ tsp mixed spice
1½ tsp rosewater
½ tsp vanilla extract
½ tsp baking powder

Takes 3¼–3½ hours • Cuts into 16 slices

1 Preheat the oven to 160°C/Gas 3/fan oven 140°C. Completely line a deep 20cm round cake tin. Beat the butter and sugar until very creamy. Stir in a spoonful of flour, then the beaten eggs and remaining flour alternately, a quarter at a time, beating well with a wooden spoon. Stir in the almonds.
2 Mix in the sherry; add the peel, cherries, raisins, currants, nuts, zest, spice, rosewater and vanilla. Stir in the baking powder.
3 Spoon into the tin, smooth the top, making a slight dip in the centre. Bake for 30 minutes. Lower temperature to 150°C/Gas 2/fan oven 130°C and bake for another 2–2¼ hours, until a skewer inserted in the middle comes out clean. Cool in tin, remove and discard lining paper. When cold, wrap well in cling film and foil and store.

• Per slice 427 kcalories, protein 7g, carbohydrate 53g, fat 22g, saturated fat 8g, fibre 2g, added sugar 17g, salt 0.42g

For a beautifully moist cake, pierce the top with a skewer and pour over 2 tablespoons bourbon every few weeks up to the big day.

Deluxe Christmas Cake

4 tbsp bourbon
225g/8oz sultanas
100g/4oz glacé cherries, halved
100g/4oz semi-dried pineapple, roughly chopped
2 pieces of stem ginger, finely chopped
500g/1lb 2oz crystallized fruits (such as oranges, pears, figs, pineapple), roughly chopped, plus extra whole fruits to decorate
100g/4oz walnuts, roughly chopped
grated zest and juice of 1 lemon
225g/8oz butter, at room temperature
225g/8oz golden caster sugar
4 large eggs, beaten
225g/8oz plain flour mixed with ½ tsp salt
ribbon, to decorate

Takes about 3¼ hours • Cuts into 12 big slices

1 Preheat the oven to 150°C/Gas 2/fan oven 130°C. Butter and double line a deep 20cm/8in round cake tin. Mix the bourbon and sultanas and let stand. Stir occasionally.
2 Put the remaining fruits and the nuts and lemon juice into a bowl. In another bowl, cream the butter, sugar and lemon zest. Add the eggs alternately with the flour in three or four batches. Stir in the sultanas plus any liquid, and all the fruit and nut mixture. Transfer to the tin and smooth the top, making a dip in the centre.
3 Bake for about 2½ hours. Cool in the tin briefly, then remove and cool fully. Wrap the cake tightly in cling film and foil. It will keep in a cool spot for up to 2 months.
4 Pile the extra, whole crystallized fruits on top and finish off with ribbon.

• Per slice 594 kcalories, protein 7g, carbohydrate 90g, fat 24g, saturated fat 11g, fibre 3g, added sugar 38g, salt 0.69g

A stylish and smart Christmas design – yet reassuringly simple to make.

Elegant Berry Wreath Cake

20–23cm/8–9in round homemade or shop-bought fruit cake

TO DECORATE
50g/2oz golden caster sugar
several eucalyptus sprigs
1 egg white, lightly beaten
plenty of fresh bay leaves, in sprigs
100g/4oz cranberries, defrosted if frozen and drained

TO COVER THE CAKE
500g pack natural marzipan
3 tbsp apricot jam

FOR THE ROYAL ICING
2 egg whites
400g/14oz icing sugar, sifted, plus extra for rolling out

Takes 30 minutes, plus overnight setting • Cuts into 12–16 slices

1 Use a 5–6cm/2–2½in round cutter to cut a hole from the centre of the cake. Put the caster sugar on a plate, dip the tips of the eucalyptus leaves into the egg white, shake off any excess, then coat in sugar. Dry.

2 Meanwhile, dust the work surface with icing sugar. Roll the marzipan to a 20 or 23cm/8 or 9in circle. Warm and sieve the jam and brush it over the top of the cake. Place it jam side down on the marzipan. Cut out a hole in the marzipan to match that in the cake, using a sharp knife or cutter. Turn the cake right way up and put on a plate.

3 Beat the egg whites and icing sugar until thick and smooth. Spread over the marzipan with a palette knife. Decorate with the berries and leaves. Let set overnight.

• Per slice for 12 554 kcalories, protein 5.6g, carbohydrate 110.4g, fat 12.9g, saturated fat 2.4g, fibre 2g, sugar 102.5g, salt 0.34g

A Christmas cake that outshines all others
and brings a sparkle to the yuletide spread.

Silver Star Cake

20cm/8in round homemade or
shop-bought fruit cake, covered
with marzipan
1kg/2lb 4oz royal icing
silver smarties
wired star garland

Takes about 30 minutes, plus
overnight setting •
Cuts into 12–16 slices

1 Put the cake on a cake board. Dab a little of the royal icing in the middle of the board and sit the cake on top. Leave it to set so it is secure on the board.

2 Spread the royal icing over the cake in swirls and peaks. Stick the silver smarties into the icing and leave overnight to set.

3 Attach the wired stars under the cake board with sticky tape (do not push the wire into the cake as it can affect it) and drape around the cake.

• Per slice for 12 668 kcalories, protein 5.2g, carbohydrate 142.9g, fat 12.1g, saturated fat 2.3g, fibre 1.6g, sugar 134.6g, salt 0.35g

Get creative and get the children involved
with this fun, festive cake.

Santa's Stocking Cake

250g/9oz white ready-to-roll white icing
pink, green and orange food colouring (or use colours of your choice)
½ quantity royal icing (see page 32 – Elegant Berry Wreath Cake)
a thin red ribbon
20cm/8in round homemade or shop-bought fruit cake, covered with marzipan and white ready-to-roll icing
orange, green and pink Smarties
3 small gift boxes (from stationers or gift shops)

Takes about 40 minutes, plus drying • Cuts into 12–16 slices

1 Knead the icing until smooth, then split into three equal pieces and colour each one. Roll out to about 5mm/¼in thickness and, using a template, cut out eight stocking shapes. Set aside on parchment paper.

2 Make the royal icing and colour. With the end of a skewer, dot small 'spots' all over the stocking shapes (or use a piping bag). Set aside to dry. Keep the coloured icing covered with cling film.

3 Fix the ribbon around the top edge of the cake, using a thin line of icing to help it stick. Place on board or plate. Using a little leftover coloured icing, 'hang' the stockings on the cake, just underneath the ribbon, in alternating colours. Top the cake with Smartie-filled boxes and scatter Smarties over the cake and board or plate.

• Per slice for 12 543 kcalories, protein 5.1g, carbohydrate 104.9g, fat 14.1g, saturated fat 2.3g, fibre 1.6g, sugar 96.8g, salt 0.33g

Perfect for the less experienced baker – this smart decoration requires no skill, just a pretty selection of colourful ribbons.

Pastel Ribbon Cake

20cm/8in round marzipan-covered homemade or shop-bought fruit cake
650g/1lb 7oz white ready-to-roll icing
ribbons of different colours and thicknesses

Takes about 35 minutes • Cuts into 12–16 slices

1 Cover the cake with the ready-to-roll icing, reserving a small piece of icing.
2 Soften the piece of icing with water and use some to secure the cake by pressing it on to the centre of a cake board. Sit the cake on top.
3 To decorate, lay and criss-cross the ribbons on the cake at right angles, securing underneath the cake with the rest of the softened icing.

• Per slice for 12 563 kcalories, protein 4.4g, carbohydrate 111.4g, fat 14g, saturated fat 2.3g, fibre 1.6g, sugar 103.3g, salt 0.34g

This sophisticated and elegant-looking cake is in fact the easiest, last-minute, no-ice decoration, filling the air with Christmas aromas.

Fragrant Spice Cake

20cm/8in round homemade or shop-bought fruit cake, covered with white marzipan
5 fresh rosemary sprigs
1 egg white, lightly beaten
caster sugar, for coating
15 fresh bay leaves
5 long cinnamon sticks
cotton thread
2m/2yd thin gold braid
extra marzipan for fixing decorations
8 star anise
1m/1yd gold ribbon, 3cm/1¼in wide
pin or double-sided sticky tape

Takes about 30 minutes • Cuts into 12–16 slices

1 Place the cake on a plate. Dip each rosemary sprig in the egg white, coat in sugar. Shake off and reserve excess sugar.
2 Make 5 fragrant bundles: gather together a rosemary sprig, 3 bay leaves and a cinnamon stick, and tie at the end with thread. Join the bundles together with the gold braid, twisting it around each bundle and leaving a length between each one.
3 Lay the bundles on the cake so they radiate from the centre, letting the thread loop loosely between each one. As you lay it down, fix each bundle to the cake with a little extra marzipan. Scatter the star anise over the cake and sprinkle some reserved sugar over the marzipan. Wrap the ribbon around the cake and secure with a pin or tape. The herb bundles will keep fresh for 3–4 days.

• Per slice for 12 382 kcalories, protein 4.6g, carbohydrate 66.7g, fat 12.4g, saturated fat 2.4g, fibre 1.7g, sugar 59.1g, salt 0.28g

Make your own white Christmas with this seasonal cake. It will keep in a cool, dry place, preferably in a tin, for up to 2 weeks.

Snowflake Cake

1 large egg white
200g/7oz icing sugar, sifted
waxed paper or baking parchment
Edible Sparkle or Glitter Flakes, for sprinkling
100g/4oz granulated sugar
20cm/8in round homemade or shop-bought fruit cake, covered with natural marzipan and white ready-to-roll icing
6–8 lengths white floristry wire, made into coils round a spice jar
4 tbsp icing sugar
4 nightlights, removed from their cases, to decorate

Takes 1¾–2 hours, plus at least a day for setting the snowflakes • Cuts into 12–16

1 Beat egg white and icing sugar until smooth. Put in a piping bag fitted with a fine nozzle. Line two baking sheets with parchment.
2 For a large snowflake, pipe a 7cm/2¾in line on the paper, cross with two more lines to make a six-pointed star. Pipe six inverted arrows along each point, growing smaller as they reach the tips. Sprinkle with Edible Sparkle, then granulated sugar. Make 3–4 more, in different sizes. Shape 12–14 smaller snowflakes: each line 3–4cm/1¼–1½in long, with 2–3 arrows on each. Set overnight.
3 Place cake on a plate. Make a paste with icing sugar and a few drops of water. Arrange nightlights on cake, decorate with coils and stars, pressing into the icing, securing with icing paste. Sprinkle more sparkle on cake.

• Per slice for 12 663 kcalories, protein 4.6g, carbohydrate 137.7g, fat 14g, saturated fat 2.3g, fibre 1.6g, sugar 129.4g, salt 0.36g

Make your mince pies extra special and rich with a touch of melt-in-the-mouth marzipan and a dusting of icing sugar.

Marzipan Mince Pies

100g/4oz plain flour
100g/4oz self-raising flour
100g/4oz butter, cut into cubes
1 tbsp caster sugar
finely grated zest 1 lemon
85g/3oz marzipan, cut into 24 pieces
250g/9oz mincemeat (just over ½ jar)
icing sugar, for dusting

Takes about 45 minutes • Makes 12 • To make ahead, freeze the pies unbaked then bake straight from the freezer for 25 minutes.

1 Preheat the oven to 200°C/Gas 6/fan oven 180°C. Process both flours and the butter in a food processor until the mixture is like fine breadcrumbs. Pulse in the sugar and zest, then 3–4 tablespoons of cold water, until dough comes together into a ball.

2 Roll the dough out thinly on a lightly floured surface. Stamp out into 9cm/3½ in rounds. (Reserve the excess pastry.) Line a 12-hole bun tin, and gather up the edges into folds.

3 Put two pieces of marzipan in the bottom of each pastry case, spoon in a heaped teaspoon of mincemeat. Roll out the pastry trimmings, cut out star shapes and lay on top. Bake for 12–15 minutes until crisp and golden. Cool in the tin then remove and cool on a wire rack. Dust with icing sugar.

• Per pie 211 kcalories, protein 2g, carbohydrate 33g, fat 9g, saturated fat 5g, fibre 1g, added sugar 15g, salt 0.33g

These delicious, crumbly mince pies are perfect served warm with brandy cream.

Crumble-Top Mince Pies

225g/8oz plain flour
100g/4oz butter, chilled and roughly cubed
3 tbsp light muscovado sugar
grated zest and juice 2 satsumas
225g/8oz mincemeat
2 tbsp flaked almonds
1 tbsp stem ginger syrup
icing sugar, for dusting

Takes 20 minutes, plus 30 minutes chilling • Makes 12

1 For the pastry, rub the flour and butter together using your fingertips until it looks like coarse breadcrumbs. Stir in the sugar and zest. Set aside 4 tablespoons of this mix. Add about 4 tablespoons of the satsuma juice to the main pastry mix to make a fairly soft dough, kneading until smooth. Wrap in cling film and chill for 30 minutes.

2 Preheat the oven to 200°C/Gas 6/fan oven 180°C. Roll out the pastry to a £1 coin thickness. Using a 9cm/3½in fluted cutter, stamp out 12 circles of pastry. Use to line individual tartlet tins, with the pastry just a little higher. Spoon in the mincemeat.

3 Sprinkle the pastry crumble mix over, then the almonds and drizzle over the ginger syrup. Bake for 18–20 minutes until golden. Cool on a wire rack. Dust with icing sugar.

• Per pie 213 kcalories, protein 2g, carbohydrate 33g, fat 9g, saturated fat 5g, fibre 1g, added sugar 14g, salt 0.26g

A creative variation on the classic mince pie.
Eat hot with vanilla ice cream, or just as they are.

Roly-Poly Mince Pies

50g/2oz golden caster sugar
1 sheet ready-rolled puff pastry
411g jar traditional mincemeat
1 tbsp milk
25g/1oz flaked almonds

Takes about 50 minutes, plus 30 minutes, chilling • Makes 12 large mince pies

1 Preheat the oven to 200°C/Gas 6/fan oven 180°C. Scatter the sugar over the worktop, unravel pastry, then roll out so it's a quarter bigger, but still rectangular.
2 Spread the mincemeat over the pastry leaving a 2cm/1¾in border along the longest edges. Fold one long edge over then roll the pastry tightly into a sausage shape, gently pressing the pastry into the mincemeat. Brush with milk and press down to seal in the mincemeat. Press both ends in to plump up the roll and chill for at least 30 minutes.
3 Cut the roll into 12×3cm/1¼in thick rounds. Lay them on a large baking sheet and flatten with your hand. Scatter the almonds over and bake for 20 30 minutes until golden brown. Cool for 5 minutes – keeping them separate to prevent sticking.

• Per pie 190 kcalories, protein 2g, carbohydrate 32g, fat 7g, saturated fat 1g, fibre 1g, added sugar 20g, salt 0.16g

A sweet treat full of festive colour
and seasonal cranberries.

Cranberry Christmas Rockies

50g/2oz unsalted butter
100g/4oz self-raising flour
1 tsp ground mixed spice
50g/2oz light muscovado sugar
85g pack dried cranberries
1 small apple, peeled, halved,
cored and finely diced
1 egg, beaten
1 tbsp milk
icing sugar, to dust

Takes 35 minutes •
Makes 8 large or 16 small pieces

1 Preheat the oven to 180°C/Gas 4/fan oven 160°C and lightly oil a large, non-stick baking sheet. Rub together the butter and flour with your fingertips to fine breadcrumbs (or pulse in a food processor).
2 Stir in the rest of the ingredients (except the icing sugar) until you have a soft dough.
3 Drop 8 tablespoons or 16 heaped teaspoons of the dough on to the baking sheet, spacing out well. Bake for 18–20 minutes until golden. Transfer to a wire rack to cool and dust with plenty of icing sugar. These are best eaten a day or two after baking.

• Per serving 16 pieces 80 kcalories, protein 1g, carbohydrate 12g, fat 3g, saturated fat 2g, fibre 1g, added sugar 3g, salt 0.1g

These biscuits are perfect for hanging as edible decorations – if they can stay on the tree that long!

Lemon Stars

FOR THE SHORTBREAD
325g/11oz plain flour
225g/8oz chilled salted butter, cut into small pieces
125g/4½oz golden caster sugar
2 tsp good-quality vanilla extract
2 egg yolks
finely grated zest of 1 lemon

FOR THE DECORATION
1 tbsp lightly beaten egg white
1 tbsp lemon juice
225g/8oz icing sugar
100g/4oz tropical dried fruits
50g/2oz dried cranberries, chopped
a small handful of silver balls
ribbon, for hanging on the tree

Takes 45–55 minutes, plus chilling • Makes 16–18 biscuits

1 Preheat the oven to 180°C/Gas 4/fan oven 160°C. Grease 2 baking sheets. Whiz flour and butter in a food processor to fine breadcrumbs. Add the sugar, vanilla, egg yolks and lemon zest and whiz to a smooth dough. Roll out (about 5mm/¼in thick), cut out star biscuits using a 10cm/4in cutter.
2 With a skewer, make a small hole 1cm/½in from a point on each star. Bake for 18–20 minutes until pale golden around edges. Cool on a wire rack. (If the holes fill in, re-make them while the biscuits are hot.)
3 Put the egg white and lemon juice in a bowl. Beat in icing sugar until smooth. Spread it generously over the middle of the biscuits. Mix the fruits, then scatter them on the icing with some silver balls. Leave to set. Thread with ribbon and eat within 24 hours.

• Per biscuit 279 kcalories, protein 3g, carbohydrate 44g, fat 11g, saturated fat 7g, fibre 1g, added sugar 22g, salt 0.26g

If there's no snow for making snowmen,
keep little hands busy in the kitchen making these cakes instead.

Snow-capped Fairy Cakes

175g/6oz butter
175g/6oz golden caster sugar
3 eggs
225g/8oz self-raising flour
finely grated zest of 1 orange
1 tsp vanilla extract
4 tbsp milk

FOR THE ICING
1 egg white
4 tbsp orange juice
175g/6oz icing sugar
fruit jellies (thinly sliced) and silver
balls, to decorate

Takes 45 minutes • Makes 18

1 Preheat the oven to 190°C/ Gas 5/fan oven 170°C. Line 18 holes of bun tins with paper cases. Melt the butter and cool for 5 minutes, tip into a large bowl with all the cake ingredients, beat for 1–2 minutes until smooth. Spoon into the cases,until three-quarters full. Bake for 15–18 minutes until lightly browned and firm. Cool on a wire rack.
2 For the icing, put the egg white and orange juice into a heatproof bowl, sift in the icing sugar, then set over a pan of simmering water. Using an electric hand whisk, whisk the icing for 7 minutes until glossy and standing in soft peaks. Remove from heat, whisk for 2 more minutes until slightly cooled.
3 Swirl the icing on to the cakes, decorate and leave to set. They will keep for 3 days.

• Per cake 210 kcalories, protein 3g, carbohydrate 31g, fat 9g, saturated fat 5g, fibre none, sugar 22g, salt 0.31g

A delicious traditional alternative to Christmas cake. It will keep for a week wrapped in double-thickness foil, or frozen for up to a month.

Chocolate Fondant Log

140g/5oz light muscovado sugar
2 tbsp water
5 eggs, separated into two bowls
100g/4oz self-raising flour, sifted
25g/1oz good-quality cocoa powder, sifted
caster sugar, for sprinkling

FOR THE ICING AND FILLING
285ml carton double cream
450g/1lb fondant chocolate, such as Lindt Lindor, broken into pieces
1 holly sprig
icing sugar, for dusting

Takes about 50 minutes, plus cooling
• Cuts into 16 slices

1 Preheat oven to 190°C/Gas 5/fan oven 170°C. Butter and line a 30×35cm/12×14in Swiss roll tin. Add sugar and water to egg yolks. Whisk until mix leaves a ribbon trail. Fold in flour and cocoa. Stiffly beat egg whites. Gradually fold into cake. Pour into tin. Bake 10–12 minutes, until cake is firm. Turn out on to parchment sprinkled with sugar, remove lining. Cover, cool. Trim edges, roll up from a long side, keeping paper inside.
2 Boil the cream, remove from heat, stir in 400g/14oz of chocolate. Chill until spreadable. Chop remaining chocolate, mix with one-third of icing to make the filling.
3 Unroll cake, spread filling over, re-roll, set on a board. Cut a diagonal slice off one end. Fix it to the large roll with icing. Decorate with remaining icing, holly and icing sugar.

• Per slice 343 kcalories, protein 5g, carbohydrate 30g, fat 24g, saturated fat 12g, fibre 2g, sugar 19g, salt 0.14g

An easy ready-rolled pastry version of a stollen. For added festive indulgence, serve slices with a dollop of brandy butter.

Stollen Slice

25g/1oz mixed peel
50g/2oz pistachio nuts, chopped
50g/2oz dried cranberries
50g/2oz raisins
1 tbsp brandy or rum
375g pack ready-rolled puff pastry
225g/8oz shop-bought or
homemade marzipan

FOR THE GLAZE
4 tbsp apricot conserve or jam
2 tbsp brandy or rum

Takes 35–40 minutes •
Cuts into 12 slices

1 Preheat the oven to 220°C/Gas 7/fan oven 200°C. Line a baking sheet with baking parchment. Mix the peel, nuts, cranberries, raisins and brandy or rum. Soak while you make the glaze. Gently heat the jam and brandy in a small pan, then bubble for 1 minute. Sieve into a bowl, cool.
2 Lay the pastry on a lightly floured work surface. Spread the fruit and nuts almost to the edges. Roll marzipan into a long sausage. Lay it along the pastry's length over the filling, 2.5cm/1in in from one edge. Roll pastry around the marzipan, join underneath.
3 Trim ends, slice into 12. Lay the slices in a ring, slightly overlapping, on the baking sheet. Bake for 15–20 minutes until golden. Brush with glaze. Cut slices. Serve warm.

• Per slice 257 kcalories, protein 3.6g, carbohydrate 34g, fat 11.8g, saturated fat 3.4g, fibre 0.6g, sugar 22.4g, salt 0.28g

A colourful Christmas cocktail
and a modern take on an old favourite, buck's fizz.

Cranberry Fizz

⅓ cranberry juice, well chilled
⅔ good sparkling white wine,
well chilled

Takes 5 minutes

1 Fill Champagne flutes with one-third cranberry juice.
2 Top up with two-thirds of sparkling white wine and serve immediately.

The perfect drink for both those who can enjoy an alcoholic tipple and for the designated drivers.

Mulled Wine and Mulled Grape Juice

500g/1lb 2oz sugar
16 cloves
3 cinnamon sticks
6 lemons, thinly sliced
3 orange zest strips
2 × 75cl bottles red wine
1.5 litres/2¾ pints red grape juice
juice of 1 lime
twists of orange and lime zest, to decorate

Takes 55 minutes • Makes 24 glasses

1 In a large pan over a moderate heat, dissolve the sugar in 1 litre/1¾ pints water. Add the spices, bring to the boil and simmer for 10 minutes. Add the lemons and orange zest. Remove from the heat and leave to stand for about 30 minutes. Strain, cool and chill.

2 Divide the sugar syrup between two pans. Add the wine to one and the grape juice and lime juice to the other. Heat gently, do not allow to boil. Serve in jugs, taking care that the liquid is not too hot. Decorate the glasses with twists of orange and lime zest on cocktail sticks.

For a non-alcoholic version, replace the water with tea and simmer for 2–3 minutes, and replace the wine with red grape juice.

Spiced Wine Punch

100g/4oz light muscovado sugar
2 oranges, zest pared, juice squeezed from one, the other cut into chunks
2 cinnamon sticks, broken in half
a little freshly grated nutmeg
1 × 75cl bottle light red wine
1 apple, quartered, cored and thickly sliced

Takes 25 minutes •
Makes 8–10 glasses

1 Put the sugar, the orange zest, juice and chunks, cinnamon and nutmeg in a pan with 300ml/½ pt water and bring to the boil.
2 Simmer for 10 minutes to infuse the spices, then add the wine and apple slices and bring to a simmer.
3 Serve in heatproof glasses.

This warm spiced wine is traditionally served in small cups
with a teaspoon, so you can eat as you drink!

Glogg

10 cardamom pods, spilt in half
2 cinnamon sticks
6 cloves
100g/4oz piece of fresh root ginger,
sliced
1 × 75cl bottle red wine
85g/3oz caster sugar
a shot of vodka
flaked almonds and raisins, to serve

Takes 25 minutes • Serves 10

1 Put the spices in a pan with the wine and sugar. Bring to the boil.
2 Simmer very gently for 5 minutes, then turn off the heat. Cover and leave to infuse for 15 minutes.
3 Pour in the vodka. Serve with a few flaked almonds and raisins in each glass.

Chicory leaves make elegant, edible spoons, as they hold their shape and crispness perfectly.

Caesar Chicory Scoops

100g/4oz unsmoked bacon lardons
1 cooked chicken breast, without skin
1 baby gem lettuce
50g/2oz ready-made croûtons, preferably small ones
4 tbsp Caesar salad dressing
2 tbsp freshly grated parmesan
16–18 medium-size chicory leaves (red and green together look stunning)
parmesan shavings, to garnish

Takes 40–50 minutes • Makes 16–18 scoops

1 Slowly fry the lardons in a small frying pan until they are crisp. Remove from the pan and leave to cool on kitchen paper to absorb any excess fat. Finely shred the chicken and lettuce. (Can be prepared two hours in advance and chilled. Put together half an hour before serving.)

2 Place chicken and lettuce in a bowl and add the croûtons, dressing, parmesan and cooled lardons. Season with some freshly milled black pepper, then mix everything gently together.

3 Spoon the Caesar salad on to the chicory leaves, leaving the base free (to act as handles). Sprinkle with parmesan shavings and grind black pepper over, then arrange on a plate and they are ready to serve.

• Per scoop 69 kcalories, protein 4g, carbohydrate 2g, fat 5g, saturated fat 1g, fibre none, added sugar none, salt 0.36

Spice up your cocktail parties and perk up traditional canapés
with this fun way to serve satay.

Satay Shots

4 skinless boneless chicken breasts
3 tbsp soy sauce
1 heaped tbsp Very Lazy chillies or
chilli sauce or paste
2 garlic cloves, crushed
1 tbsp vegetable oil
1 heaped tbsp light muscovado
sugar
415g jar ready-made satay sauce
1 lime, cut in half
12 lime slices

Takes 20–30 minutes • Makes 36
skewers

1 Cut the chicken breasts into 36 thin strips
and put them into a bowl with the soy sauce,
chillies (or sauce or paste), garlic, oil and
sugar. Mix together until the chicken is
coated, then thread each strip on to a
bamboo skewer. Get the skewers lined up
on a baking sheet and keep covered in the
fridge until ready to cook.
2 Preheat the oven to 190°C/Gas 5/fan oven
170°C. Put the sheet in the hottest part of
the oven for 10 minutes. Meanwhile, warm
the satay sauce in a pan, then spoon
amongst 12 shot glasses or small tumblers.
3 When the chicken is done, remove from
the oven and squeeze over the lime juice.
Pop 3 skewers in each shot glass and a lime
slice on to each rim. Serve warm or cold.

• Per skewer 89 kcalories, protein 6g, carbohydrate
3g, fat 6g, saturated fat 1g, fibre 1g, added sugar 2g,
salt 0.53g

Roast potatoes are always a crowd pleaser,
but to add a simple kick, try them with any bought pesto.

Pesto Roast Potatoes

1.3kg/3lb small new potatoes
4 tbsp olive oil
2 tbsp pesto
cocktail sticks, to serve

Takes 55 minutes •
Serves 12 (4 small potatoes each)

1 Preheat the oven to 200°C/Gas 6/fan oven 180°C. Spread the potatoes in a roasting tin, pour over the oil and stir to coat.
2 Bake for 45 minutes until golden and tender. Drain then toss with the pesto.
3 Serve with a bowl of coarse sea salt and little bowls of cocktail sticks, so your guests can spear the potatoes for themselves.

• Per serving 117 kcalories, protein 2.4g, carbohydrate 17.5g, fat 4.7g, saturated fat 0.8g, fibre 1.1g, sugar 1.4g, salt 0.06g

Quick and easy to prepare, these canapés are best made to order as they soften if allowed to stand around too long.

Spicy Prawn Poppadums

24 cooked and peeled extra large tiger prawns, thawed if frozen
24 ready-to-eat mini poppadums, plain or assorted
200g tub tzatziki
a little chopped fresh coriander
paprika, for dusting

Takes 10–15 minutes • Makes 24 poppadums

1 Dry the prawns on kitchen paper and keep covered in the fridge. Lay the poppadums out on a serving platter.
2 Spoon a little tzatziki into each poppadum. Stand a prawn on top, then finish with a scattering of coriander and a light dusting of paprika.

• Per poppadum 58 kcalories, protein 5g, carbohydrate 4g, fat 2g, saturated fat none, fibre none, added sugar none, salt 0.92g

Turn a jar of artichoke hearts and a handful of mint
into a great little dip in a moment.

Artichoke and Mint Dip

285g jar artichoke antipasto in oil
a good handful of mint leaves,
stripped from the stalks
3 tbsp crème fraîche
1–2 tsp lemon juice
6 pitta breads
2 tbsp olive oil
a scattering of Maldon sea salt
lemon wedge and mint sprig,
to garnish

Takes 15–20 minutes • Serves 6–8

1 Blitz the artichokes and their oil with the mint in a food processor until fairly smooth. Add the crème fraîche, season and briefly pulse, then add lemon juice to taste. Tip into a small bowl, cover and chill.
2 Preheat the oven to 200°C/Gas 6/fan oven 180°C. Tear the pittas into rough pieces and spread over a couple of baking sheets. Drizzle with olive oil and scatter over some sea salt. Bake for 7–10 minutes until crisp.
3 Set the bowl of dip on a large platter and garnish with a lemon wedge and a sprig of mint. Surround with the crisp pitta pieces.

• Per serving for 6 362 kcalories, protein 7g, carbohydrate 38g, fat 21g, saturated fat 4g, fibre 2g, added sugar none, salt 1.34g

Make a start on the Christmas Stilton
with these cheesey canapés.

Crunchy Christmas Crostini

1 ready-to-bake ciabatta loaf
1 tbsp olive oil
1 large wedge Stilton, about
225g/8oz, used from the fridge
about ½ a 290g jar salad beetroot
pickle, or other pickle or chutney
a handful of celery leaves taken from
the middle of a head of celery

Takes 25–35 minutes • Makes 25
crostini

1 Preheat the oven to 200°C/Gas 6/fan oven 180°C. Slice the ciabatta into about 25 thin slices. Lay them on a couple of baking sheets and brush with the oil. Toast in the oven for 10 minutes until golden, checking after 5 minutes and turning if necessary. Cut the Stilton into slices a little smaller than the toasts. (Can be prepared and covered up to 1 hour ahead.)

2 Spoon a little pile of beetroot on to the end of each piece of bread. Prop a slice of cheese up against each pile of beetroot and bake for 3–4 minutes until the cheese is starting to melt. You don't want it too melty – try to catch it just as it's starting to ooze over the edge.

3 Top each cheesey canapé with a little sprig of celery leaves and serve immediately.

• Per crostini 62 kcalories, protein 3g, carbohydrate 5g, fat 4g, saturated fat 2g, fibre none, added sugar none, salt 0.4g

This scrumptious breadstick
is the perfect nibble for pizza lovers.

Tomato Breadsticks

290g box pizza dough
100g/4oz SunBlush or sun-dried
tomatoes in oil, finely chopped
beaten egg, for glazing

Takes 40 minutes • Makes about 20
breadsticks

1 Make up the pizza-dough mix according to pack instructions, using all of the mix. Cover with oiled cling film and set aside for 10 minutes.
2 Preheat the oven to 200°C/Gas 6/fan oven 180°C and dust two baking sheets with flour. Tip the dough on to a floured work surface and knead. Drain the SunBlush or sun-dried tomatoes in oil and finely chop. Knead into the dough, then roll out the dough to a rectangle about 18×24cm/7×9½ in. Cut into 4 lengthways, then cut each piece into 5 long strips. Roll each strip a little longer, then place on the baking sheets, 2cm/¾ in apart.
3 Brush with beaten egg and bake for 10–15 minutes until golden. Transfer to a rack. Can be made up to 2 days ahead. Re-crisp in a hot oven before serving.

• Per stick 51 kcalories, protein 2g, carbohydrate 9g, fat 1g, saturated fat none, fibre 1g, sugar 1g, salt 0.42g

Stylish, delicious and deceptively simple,
these crab bites will wow your guests.

Curried Thai Crab Bites

50g/2oz mayonnaise
1 tbsp red or green Thai curry paste
100g pack bite-size Thai rice cakes
a handful of coriander leaves, plus
extra whole leaves
250g/9oz white crabmeat

Takes 15 minutes • Makes 40 canapés

1 Mix the mayonnaise with the Thai curry paste. Spoon a small amount on to bite-size Thai rice cakes (use a whole 100g pack).
2 Finely chop the handful of coriander leaves and mix with the crabmeat. Season to taste.
3 To serve, spoon a little crabmeat on to the mayonnaise and decorate with more whole coriander leaves.

• Per canapé 17 kcalories, protein 1g, carbohydrate 1g, fat 1g, saturated fat none, fibre none, sugar none, salt 0.12g

The perfect winter warmer – divinely comforting.

Mini Chilli Beef Pies

450g pack ready-rolled shortcrust pastry sheets

FOR THE QUICK CHILLI
1 tbsp sunflower oil
1 small onion, chopped
2 tsp hot chilli powder
2 tsp ground cumin
250g/9oz beef mince
85g/3oz tomato purée
150ml/¼ pt beef stock
a large pinch of ground cinnamon
200g/8oz kidney beans, drained and rinsed

FOR THE MASH
1 large potato (about 250g/9oz), peeled, cut into chunks
3 tbsp soured cream
2 tbsp chopped chives

Takes 1 hour 25 minutes • Makes 24

1 For the chilli, heat oil in a pan, fry onion until soft. Add spices and fry 1 minute. Stir in beef, cook for a few minutes. Stir in tomato purée, stock and cinnamon, bring to the boil, then simmer for 15–20 minutes until very little liquid is left. Add beans 5 minutes before end of cooking. Season, cool.

2 Preheat the oven to 200°C/Gas 6/fan oven 180°C. Using a 7cm/2¾ in cutter, cut 12 pastry circles and line a 12-hole mini muffin tray. Prick pastry bases with a fork, bake 10 minutes. Remove from oven, cool on a wire rack. Repeat with remaining pastry.

3 Cook the potato in boiling water until tender. Drain, mash with soured cream, stir in chives. Spoon 1–2 teaspoons of chilli into the pastry cases. Top with mash. Return to oven for 15 minutes until golden.

• Per serving 137 kcalories, protein 4g, carbohydrate 13g, fat 8g, saturated fat 3g, fibre 1g, added sugar 1g, salt 0.33g

A taste of the Mediterranean, and the perfect light bite.

Rosemary and Olive Drop Scones with Goats' Cheese

225g/8oz self-raising flour
1 tsp baking powder
2 eggs, beaten
200ml/7fl oz milk
1 sprig rosemary, leaves removed and finely chopped
a handful of black olives, stoned and chopped
sunflower oil, for frying
175g/6oz firm goats' cheese, sliced in small pieces
200g punnet cherry tomatoes, halved
extra virgin olive oil and black pepper, to serve

Takes 45 minutes • Makes 24

1 Sieve the flour and baking powder into a large bowl and season. Make a well in the middle. Pour in the eggs and a splash of the milk then start to beat the mix until smooth, stirring in the rest of the milk to make a smooth batter. Mix in the rosemary and olives.
2 Warm a lightly oiled non-stick frying pan. Cook a tablespoon of the mix for 2 minutes or until golden underneath. Flip over and fry for another minute then cool. Do this in 3 or 4 batches (greasing the pan in between).
3 Heat grill to high. Place the drop scones on a baking sheet. Arrange the cheese on top of each one. Top with the tomatoes and grill for 5 minutes to melt the cheese and heat the tomatoes. Serve with a grinding of pepper and a drizzle of olive oil.

• Per scone 66 kcalories, protein 3g, carbohydrate 7g, fat 3g, saturated fat 2g, fibre none, added sugar none, salt 0.31g

Delectably simple roast that looks smart served with stuffing balls
and sausages and garnished with bay leaves.

Classic Roast Turkey with Red Wine Baste

1 onion, peeled and quartered
fresh bay sprig and leaves,
to flavour and serve
4.5–5.6kg/10–12lb Bronze turkey,
giblets removed
1 quantity of your favourite stuffing
85g/3oz butter, softened
1 whole nutmeg
10 rashers streaky bacon
1 glass red wine, such as Merlot
extra stuffing balls and sausages
wrapped in bacon, to serve
salt and pepper, to season

Takes 20 minutes, plus 3–3½ hours
cooking • Serves 8–10 with leftovers
(Calculate turkey cooking time at 20
minutes per kilo, plus 90 minutes)

1 Preheat the oven to 190°C/Gas 5/fan oven 170°C. Put onion and bay sprig in the cavity between the turkey legs. Pack stuffing into the neck end. Secure neck end flap with skewers, tie legs together. Weigh turkey and calculate cooking time as left.
2 Lay turkey in a roasting tin. Smear with the butter, grate over half the nutmeg, season. Cover breast with bacon, pour over the wine, cover with a loose tent of foil.
3 Roast for calculated time. About 90 minutes before the end, open the foil, discard bacon and fat, then continue roasting until brown, basting several times. To test if cooked, push a skewer into thickest part of the thigh – the juices should run clear. Transfer turkey to a platter, cover with foil, let rest 20–30 minutes.

• Per serving 476 kcalories, protein 74g, carbohydrate none, fat 19g, saturated fat 7g, fibre none, sugar none, salt 0.69g

Spice up the Christmas roast with this crunchy combination
of crushed seeds and seasoning.

Roast Turkey with Crushed Spices

1 onion, peeled and halved
4.5–5.6kg/10lb–12lb turkey,
thawed if frozen, giblets removed
1 quantity of your favourite stuffing
50g/2oz butter
1 tbsp each coriander seeds,
mustard seeds and mixed
coloured peppercorns,
coarsely crushed
coarse salt, to season
roast potatoes and extra stuffing
balls, to serve
fresh coriander sprigs, to garnish

Takes 10 minutes, plus 3–3½ hours
cooking time • Serves 10–12

1 Preheat the oven to 190°C/Gas 5/fan oven 170°C. Put the onion in the bird's cavity. Stuff the neck end, secure flap with skewers and tie legs together. Weigh, and calculate cooking time (see page 88).

2 Grease a large roasting tin with some of the butter. Spread the rest over the turkey, then press in the crushed seeds. Season with salt. Put the turkey in the tin, cover loosely with foil and roast for the calculated time. Check every hour and baste carefully. One hour before the end of cooking, remove the foil, drain off any excess fat.

3 Test if cooked (see page 88). Transfer turkey to platter, cover tightly with foil. Let rest 20–30 minutes. Serve surrounded with potatoes and stuffing balls, garnished with coriander sprigs.

• Per serving for 10 546 kcalories, protein 64.2g, carbohydrate 14.6g, fat 26.1g, saturated fat 9.2g, fibre 0.7g, sugar 2g, salt 2.61g

Give your turkey a Mediterranean flavour this Christmas by covering it with fragrant herbs and crispy prosciutto.

Mediterranean Turkey

50g/2oz softened butter mixed with
2 finely chopped garlic cloves
good handful of basil leaves, torn
3 tbsp chopped flat-leaf parsley
1 tbsp chopped oregano
4.5–5kg oven-ready turkey, thawed if frozen, giblets removed
1 quantity of your favourite stuffing
1 lemon, quartered
8 slices prosciutto
roasted lemon wedges, halved garlic bulbs and fresh herbs, to garnish

FOR THE GRAVY
1 rounded tbsp plain flour
1 tbsp wholegrain mustard
1 rounded tbsp redcurrant jelly
450ml/16fl oz turkey or chicken stock
150ml/¼ pint marsala

Takes 15 minutes, plus 3–3½ hours cooking • Serves 8–10

1 Preheat oven to 190°C/Gas 5/fan oven 170°C. Mix garlic butter with herbs. Stuff neck end of turkey with stuffing, securing the flap with a skewer. Put lemon inside the turkey cavity. Spread butter over the bird. Weigh it and calculate cooking time (see page 88). Tie legs together. Put turkey in roasting tin. Cover with loose tent of foil and roast, basting every hour.
2 Remove foil 1 hour before end of cooking time, lay prosciutto over 20 minutes before end. Test (see page 88), transfer to platter and cover with foil. Rest for 20–30 minutes.
3 For gravy, spoon off excess fat from pan juices. Put roasting tin on hob, reheat. Whisk in flour, cook 2–3 minutes. Stir in mustard, redcurrant jelly, stock and marsala, bring to boil, simmer 15 minutes. Add garnish.

• Per serving for 8 779 kcalories, protein 85.9g, carbohydrate 23.9g, fat 36.5g, saturated fat 12.9g, fibre 1.6g, sugar 6.4g, salt 2.08g

This clever trick is one often used by restaurants, and it makes carving the turkey for a group so easy.

Turkey Roll

4 fresh bay leaves
4 garlic cloves
20g/¾oz dried porcini mushrooms
100ml/3½fl oz dry sherry (fino) or dry white wine
7 rashers bacon
2 large skinless turkey breasts (about 900g/2lb)
400ml/14fl oz chicken stock
1 tbsp soy sauce
salt and freshly grated black pepper, to season

Takes 1¾ hours • Serves 6

1 Preheat the oven to 200°C/ Gas 6/fan oven 180°C. Roughly chop the bay leaves, garlic and the mushrooms, then tip into a bowl and season with a pinch of salt. Pour over the sherry or wine and stir.

2 Lay the bacon on a large piece of buttered foil. Place a turkey breast on top (it should cover the bacon), spoon over the garlic mix and sandwich with the other breast. Season well and wrap up tightly like a Christmas cracker. (The turkey roll can be chilled for 24 hours.)

3 Roast for 1½ hours or until cooked. Rest for 10 minutes before carving. Meanwhile make the gravy, simmer the stock and soy sauce together with the juices from the turkey. Serve with the turkey.

• Per serving 239 kcalories, protein 45.4g, carbohydrate 3.5g, fat 3.8g, saturated fat 1.1g, fibre 0.3g, sugar 0.5g, salt 2.98g

A nifty two-in-one recipe – it's both the stuffing for the turkey
and the bacon-wrapped sausages that everyone loves.

Lightly-spiced Christmas Stuffing

225g/8oz white bread (about 5 thick
slices, crusts included)
1 large onion, peeled and quartered
2 garlic cloves
a large handful of parsley
450g/1lb good-quality sausagemeat
2 Cox's apples, cored, peeled and
finely chopped
3 celery sticks, strings removed and
diced
100g pack walnut pieces, chopped
1 tsp curry powder
1 large egg, slightly beaten
grated zest of 1 lemon and
juice of ½ lemon
20 rashers rindless streaky bacon
salt and freshly grated black
pepper, to season

Takes 1¾–2 hours • Makes enough to
stuff a 4.5–5.6kg/10–12lb turkey, plus
20 stuffing sausages

1 Whiz the bread in a food processor to
make crumbs. Tip into a large bowl. Put the
onion, garlic and parsley in the processor and
whiz until finely chopped. Add the onion mix
to the breadcrumbs with all the other
ingredients except the bacon. Season
generously and squish everything together
with your hands until combined.

2 Use about one-third of the stuffing to stuff
the neck end of the turkey and divide the rest
into 20 pieces. Mould each piece into a little
finger-sized sausage, then wrap each one in
a rasher of bacon. Put the sausages into
a shallow ovenproof dish ready for cooking.

3 To cook, once your turkey is cooked and
while it is resting, set the oven to 200°C/
Gas 6/fan oven 180°C and roast the
sausage-shaped stuffing for 30 minutes.

• Per sausage 119 kcalories, protein 6g, carbohydrate
6g, fat 8g, saturated fat 3g, fibre 1g, added sugar
none, salt 0.81g

Use plain high-quality sausagemeat, preferably made with free-range pork, and only the minimum of seasonings.

Chestnut, Bacon and Cranberry Stuffing

100g/4oz dried cranberries
50ml/2fl oz ruby port
1 small onion, peeled and chopped
2 rashers unsmoked back bacon,
cut into strips
50g/2oz butter
2 garlic cloves, chopped
450g/1lb good-quality sausagemeat
140g/5oz fresh white or brown
breadcrumbs
2 tbsp chopped fresh parsley
½ tsp chopped fresh thyme leaves
140g/5oz peeled, cooked chestnuts,
roughly chopped
1 medium egg, lightly beaten
salt and freshly grated black pepper,
to season

Takes 30–40 minutes, plus an hour to soak the cranberries • Makes about 24 stuffing balls or enough to stuff a 4.5–5.6kg/10–12lb turkey

1 Soak the cranberries in the port for an hour. Fry the onion and bacon gently in the butter, until the onion is tender and the bacon is cooked. Add the garlic and fry for another minute or so.

2 Remove from heat and cool, then mix with all the remaining ingredients, including the cranberries and port, adding enough egg to bind – hands are easiest for this. (To check seasoning, fry a knob of stuffing in a little butter, taste and adjust if necessary.)

3 Use to stuff the neck end of the turkey, or shape into 4cm/1½in round balls. To cook the stuffing balls, half an hour before the end of the turkey's cooking time, put them into the tin around the turkey or cook them in a separate, oiled tin.

• Per stuffing ball 123 kcalories, protein 4g, carbohydrate 12g, fat 7g, saturated fat 3g, fibre 1g, added sugar none, salt 0.65g

A sweet and spicy stuffing full of eastern flavours – perfect to serve with goose.

Apricot and Coriander Stuffing

2 tbsp olive oil
½ large onion, peeled and finely chopped
2 celery sticks, finely chopped
1 tsp ground coriander
250g/9oz lean minced pork
140g/5oz fresh granary or wholemeal breadcrumbs
85g/3oz ready-to-eat dried apricots, finely chopped
finely grated zest 1 large orange
3 tbsp chopped fresh parsley
2 tbsp chopped fresh mint
salt and freshly grated black pepper, to season

Takes 20 minutes • Makes enough to stuff a 4.5kg/10lb goose (see page 162 Christmas roast goose)

1 Heat the oil in a frying pan, add the onion, celery and coriander and fry gently, stirring for 10 minutes until softened but not browned.
2 Transfer to a large bowl and leave to cool. Add the remaining stuffing ingredients, plus the salt and plenty of pepper. Use your hands to mix well, squeezing the mixture so the ingredients bind together evenly.
3 Use to stuff a goose, or shape into balls. Half an hour before the end of the turkey's cooking time, put the balls into the tin around the turkey or cook them in a separate, oiled tin.

• Per serving for 6 171 kcalories, protein 12.3g, carbohydrate 17.5g, fat 6.2g, saturated fat 1.2g, fibre 2g, sugar 6.6g, salt 0.21g

Use to stuff the bird, shape into balls,
or press into a loaf tin and serve in slices.

Herb and Sausagemeat Stuffing

50g/2oz butter
2 onions, peeled and chopped
8 rashers rindless streaky bacon,
chopped
350g/12oz good-quality
sausagemeat
250g/9oz fresh white breadcrumbs
a good handful of chopped parsley
2 tbsp fresh sage or 2 tsp dried
3 tbsp chopped fresh thyme or
2 tsp dried
1 egg, beaten
1 bay leaf, optional
salt and freshly grated black
pepper, to season

Takes 55 minutes • Serves 10–12

1 Melt the butter in a pan, then fry the onions with the bacon for about 8 minutes until they are softened and golden.

2 Put the sausagemeat in a bowl with the breadcrumbs, herbs (except bay, if using) and egg. Season well. Add the onion and bacon and stir. Leave to cool.

3 To stuff the turkey, push half into the neck end, then shape the remainder into balls. Half an hour before the end of the turkey's cooking time, put the balls into the tin around the turkey or cook them in a separate, oiled tin. Alternatively, lay a bay leaf in the bottom of a 900g/2lb loaf tin, press the stuffing well in, turn it out on to a lightly oiled baking sheet, then cook with the turkey for 30 minutes.

• Per serving for 10 297 kcalories, protein 11g, carbohydrate 26g, fat 17g, saturated fat 7g, fibre 2g, added sugar none, salt 1.9g

You can shape this versatile stuffing into small balls and cook around the bird or make this fabulous-looking cake.

Sausage-nut Stuffing Cake

2 tbsp olive oil
25g/1oz butter
3 shallots, peeled and finely chopped
2 sticks celery, finely chopped
100g/4oz white breadcrumbs
500g/1lb 2oz good-quality sausagemeat
50g/2oz roughly chopped walnuts, plus extra to garnish
grated zest 1 small orange
1 tbsp chopped fresh sage leaves, or 1 tsp dried
1 egg, beaten
8 rashers rindless streaky bacon
a handful of chopped parsley, to serve

Takes about 1 hour • Serves 8–10

1 Preheat the oven to 200°C/Gas 6/fan oven 180°C. Heat the oil and butter and lightly fry the shallots and celery for 5 minutes. Tip into a bowl, add the breadcrumbs, sausagemeat, walnuts, orange zest and sage. Season, and mix together with the egg.

2 Lay the bacon up the sides of a 18–20cm/ 7–8in springform cake tin so only the ends lie on the base and the excess hangs over the edge. Carefully fill with the stuffing, level the top. Fold the bacon over the stuffing, twisting loosely into the centre. Scatter over and lightly press in the remaining walnuts.

3 Put the tin on a baking sheet. Bake for 40–45 minutes until golden. Cool in the tin for 10 minutes, turn out, scatter with parsley.

• Per serving 350 kcalories, protein 15g, carbohydrate 14g, fat 27g, saturated fat 9g, fibre 1g, added sugar none, salt 2g

The flavour of Brussels is mellowed with a citrus-nut butter
that you can tuck away in the fridge a few days ahead.

Brussels with Hazelnut and Orange Butter

85g/3oz butter, softened
finely grated zest 1 small orange
50g/2oz toasted chopped hazelnuts
1.25kg/2lb 12oz Brussels sprouts,
trimmed and halved
340g packet frozen petits pois
salt and freshly grated black pepper,
to season

Takes 20–30 minutes • Serves 10

1 Mix the butter, orange zest and hazelnuts in a small bowl with some freshly ground black pepper. (This can be done 2–3 days ahead and kept covered in the fridge.)
2 Put the sprouts into a pan of boiling salted water, bring back to the boil, cover and cook for 4–5 minutes. Add the peas and cook for a further 2 minutes. The sprouts should be only just cooked. Drain.
3 Put the sprouts and peas back into the pan and toss with the flavoured butter so it melts in. Season with salt and pepper and tip into a warmed serving dish.

• Per serving 156 kcalories, protein 6g, carbohydrate 7g, fat 12g, saturated fat 5g, fibre 6g, added sugar none, salt 0.49g

You need only a small spoonful of this as it is rich with cream. Make it a day ahead and it only needs reheating in the oven on the day.

Winter Roots Mash with Buttery Crumbs

650g/1lb 7oz parsnips, peeled and cut into even chunks
650g/1lb 7oz swede, peeled and cut into chunks as parsnips
142ml tub soured cream
1 rounded tbsp hot horseradish
2 tbsp fresh thyme leaves, plus extra for garnish
butter for greasing
25g/1oz parmesan, coarsely grated

FOR THE BUTTER TOPPING
50g/2oz butter
1 small onion, peeled and finely chopped
50g/2oz fresh white breadcrumbs
a small handful of thyme leaves, plus extra for scattering

Takes 1¼ hours–1 hour 40 minutes •
Serves 10, with other veg

1 In a large pan of boiling salted water, cook the parsnips and swede for about 20 minutes until tender. Drain, then mash until smooth. Stir in the soured cream, horseradish and thyme and season. Spoon into a buttered, shallow ovenproof dish. Set aside.
2 Make the topping. Melt the butter in a frying pan and cook the onion for 5–6 minutes, until golden. Mix in the breadcrumbs and stir to brown lightly and crisp. Season and add the thyme. Take the pan off the heat. Spoon the mixture over the mash. Scatter over the parmesan. (Can be made a day ahead and kept covered in the fridge.)
3 Preheat the oven to 190°C/Gas 5/fan oven 170°C and bake for 35–40 minutes if doing from cold 25–30 minutes if not – until golden and crisp. Serve scattered with more thyme.

• Per serving 158 kcalories, protein 4g, carbohydrate 17g, fat 9g, saturated fat 5g, fibre 5g, added sugar none, salt 0.57g

Use good-quality maple syrup to add an extra-sweet edge to carrots.

Maple-Mustard Glazed Carrots

1.3kg/3lb carrots

FOR THE MAPLE GLAZE
50g/2oz butter
1 tbsp maple syrup
1 rounded tbsp wholegrain mustard
salt and freshly grated black pepper, to season

Takes 15–20 minutes • Serves 10

1 Peel and cut the carrots into sticks. (You can do this up to 24 hours ahead and keep them in a polythene bag in the fridge.) Tip them into a pan, pour in enough boiling water just to cover, bring back to the boil, then put a lid on the pan and cook for 4–5 minutes until the carrots are just tender.
2 Meanwhile, put the butter and maple syrup in a small pan. Heat until the butter is melted then stir in the mustard. Take off the heat. Drain the carrots and tip into a warmed serving dish.
3 Pour the warm maple glaze over the carrots. Taste and adjust seasoning to suit.

• Per serving 90 kcalories, protein 1g, carbohydrate 11g, fat 5g, saturated fat 3g, fibre 3g, added sugar 1g, salt 0.3g

Fragrant herbs and light olive oil give these crunchy,
golden roast potatoes a Mediterranean flavour.

Herby Slashed Roasties

2.25kg/5lb floury potatoes, such as
Maris Piper, unpeeled, cut into
halves or quarters, depending
on size
10 small bay leaves
a handful of fresh thyme sprigs
2 tbsp butter
2 tbsp light olive oil
salt and freshly grated black
pepper, to season

Takes about 1½ hours •
Serves 8 generously

1 Bring a large pan of water to the boil and
preheat the oven to 190°C/Gas 5/fan oven
170°C. Tip the potatoes into the pan, let the
heat come back up, then boil for 6–10
minutes until just starting to soften around
the edges. Drain and return to the pan.
With the lid on, shake the potatoes until the
edges fluff up.
2 Let the potatoes cool enough to handle.
Slash half the chunks once with a small knife
and stuff alternately with bay or thyme.
3 Heat the butter and oil in a large roasting
pan either in the oven or on the hob until the
butter turns golden. Carefully tip in the
potatoes and gently turn in the fat (tongs are
best for this). Sprinkle with black pepper and
roast for 1–1¼ hours until crisp and golden,
turning halfway through. Season with sea salt.

• Per serving 266 kcalories, protein 6g, carbohydrate
49g, fat 7g, saturated fat 2g, fibre 4g, added sugar
none, salt 0.11g

To boil or not to boil? This foolproof recipe will ensure your roast potatoes are perfect on the big day.

Perfect Roast Potatoes

16 potatoes (about 2.5kg/5½lb), preferably Desirée, or Maris Piper or King Edward, peeled and halved, quartered or left whole, depending on size
2 tbsp plain flour
140g/5oz goose or duck fat or pork or beef dripping
3 tbsp sunflower or vegetable oil

Takes 1 hour 20 minutes • Serves 8

1 Preheat the oven to 190°C/Gas 5/fan oven 170°C. Tip the potatoes into a pan, cover with cold water, then bring to the boil. Boil for exactly 2 minutes. Drain, then toss in a colander to fluff up their surfaces, sprinkling over the flour as you go.
2 Place a large, sturdy roasting tray over a fairly high heat, then tip in the fat and oil. When sizzling, carefully add the potatoes. Lightly brown them in the hot fat for about 5 minutes, turning to coat with oil.
3 Roast for 20 minutes, then remove from the oven and gently turn them over. Place the tray on the hob to heat the oil, return to the oven and cook for another 20 minutes. Turn again, putting the tray back on the hob to heat the oil. Roast in the oven for another 20 minutes.

• Per serving 224 kcalories, protein 3g, carbohydrate 20g, fat 15g, saturated fat 6g, fibre 1g, added sugar 1g, salt 0.02g

Get going with this three-in-one recipe and peel, chop and freeze the veg up to a month ahead – just toss the celeriac in lemon juice first.

Pepper and Honey-Roasted Roots

3 tbsp olive oil
5 medium carrots, peeled and cut into long slices
1 large celeriac, peeled and cut into uneven chunks and wedges
5 parsnips, peeled and cut into long sticks
2 tbsp clear honey
2 tsp black peppercorns, roughly cracked

Takes 1 hour • Serves 8

1 Preheat the oven to 220°C/Gas 7/fan oven 200°C. Heat the oil in a roasting tin on top of the stove and, when it's hot, add the vegetables and fry for 5–8 minutes until they begin to brown.
2 Place the tin in the oven for 40–50 minutes, shaking it occasionally until the vegetables are golden brown and soft.
3 Stir the honey, pepper and a sprinkling of salt into the vegetables, then return to the oven for 5 minutes to warm the honey through before serving.

• Per serving 129 kcalories, protein 3g, carbohydrate 19g, fat 5, saturated fat 1g, fibre 7g, added sugar 3g, salt 1.19g

A dish bound to convert the most hardened opponents of sprouts!

Stir-fried Sprouts, Bacon and Chestnuts

16 rashers streaky bacon, cut into large chunks
250g vacuum pack peeled chestnuts
3 garlic cloves, finely sliced
1kg/2lb 4oz Brussels sprouts, trimmed and thickly sliced
100ml/3½ fl oz hot chicken stock
finely grated zest 1 lemon
a splash of soy sauce

Takes 30 minutes • Serves 8

1 Gently fry the bacon in a dry wok or large frying pan for 10 minutes until it's crispy and a lot of fat has been released.
2 Throw in the chestnuts, then continue to fry until cooked in the fat. Add the garlic, then cook until golden. Stir in the sprouts, turn up the heat, then continue to stir fry for 1 minute.
3 Pour over the stock and cook for 10 minutes until the sprouts are just cooked. Add the lemon zest and soy sauce, cook for 1 minute more then serve.

• Per serving 219 kcalories, protein 12, carbohydrate 17g, fat 12, saturated fat 4, fibre 7g, added sugar none, salt 1.44g

Improve the favours of red cabbage by making it
days in advance.

Ruby Braised Cabbage and Beetroot

50g/2oz butter
2 star anise
2 cinnamon sticks
1 large onion (a red onion
blends in, but it's not essential),
peeled and sliced
5 medium raw beetroot, peeled and
sliced into thick rounds
1 large red cabbage, leaves finely
shredded
3 tbsp sugar
100ml/3½fl oz red wine vinegar
grated zest and juice 1 orange
2 Bramley apples, peeled, cored and
roughly sliced
6 tbsp freshly grated horseradish
a handful of parsley leaves, chopped

Takes 2 hours • Serves 8

1 Melt the butter in a large pan until sizzling. Add the star anise and cinnamon, then sizzle for a few minutes. Tip in the onion, beetroot and cabbage, sprinkle over the sugar, then pour in the vinegar and orange juice. Season generously, then give everything a good stir. Cover the pan and cook over a low heat for 45 minutes, stirring occasionally.
2 Stir the apples in with cabbage, then cook for a further 35–45 minutes until the cabbage is soft. (The cabbage may be cooked up to this point and chilled for 2 days or frozen for up to 1 month.)
3 Stir half the horseradish into the cabbage and transfer to a serving dish. Mix the remaining horseradish with the parsley and orange zest and scatter the herby mixture over the cabbage before serving.

• Per serving 126 kcalories, protein 2g, carbohydrate 18g, fat 6g, saturated fat 3g, fibre 4g, added sugar 6g, salt 0.18g

If your oven is bursting at the seams and the hob is hot and bothered, cooking veg in the microwave is the ideal solution.

Buttery Leeks, Peas and Onions

50g/2oz butter
4 bay leaves
24 pearl onions or small shallots, peeled but left whole
6 large leeks, trimmed, washed and each sliced into 4 pointy chunks
150ml/¼pt vegetable or chicken stock
250g/9oz frozen peas
a bunch of fresh tarragon, roughly chopped
salt and freshly grated black pepper, to season

Takes 25–30 minutes • Serves 8

1 Tip the butter, bay leaves and onions into a large, shallow, microwaveable dish, then zap in the microwave on High for 6–8 minutes until the onions are soft, giving them a stir halfway through.
2 Stir the leeks in, pour over the stock, then cover the dish with cling film. Pierce the cling film a few times and microwave on High for 12–15 minutes until the leeks are soft.
3 Remove the cling film and stir in the frozen peas. Return to the microwave for 1 minute. Season as you like, stir in the tarragon, then serve.

• Per serving 99 kcalories, protein 4g, carbohydrate 7g, fat 6g, saturated fat 3g, fibre 5g, added sugar none, salt 0.20g

The perfect seasonal side dish to serve with roasted game or to toss through a few wintry leaves for a warm salad.

Fried Jerusalem Artichokes with Walnuts

850g/1lb 14oz Jerusalem artichokes
5 tbsp olive oil
1 tsp golden caster sugar
85g/3oz walnut halves
1 fat garlic clove, finely chopped
a handful of parsley leaves, chopped
salt and freshly grated black pepper, to season

Takes 35 minutes • Serves 4 (easily doubled)

1 Peel the artichokes with a small knife and slice them into chunks. Cook in a pan of boiling water for about 5 minutes, until just tender, then drain.

2 Heat the oil in a heavy frying pan and sauté the artichokes for 10 minutes or until golden.

3 Stir in the sugar, season with salt and pepper, then add the walnut halves. Continue to cook until the walnuts are toasted, then toss in the garlic and parsley and serve.

• Per serving 433 kcalories, protein 8g, carbohydrate 40g, fat 28g, saturated fat 3g, fibre 4g, sugar 5g, salt 0.03g

The tian cooks better if made in shallow layers in two dishes – if you prepare it a day ahead, just add the liquid an hour before cooking.

Tian of Root Vegetables

2 small sweet potatoes
2 medium potatoes
1 small celeriac, about 300g/10oz
2 small parsnips
4 tbsp olive oil, plus extra for greasing
2–3 tbsp chopped fresh parsley, plus extra to garnish
salt and freshly grated black pepper, to season

Takes 1 hour 40 minutes • Serves 12 (easily halved)

1 Preheat the oven to 200°C/Gas 6/fan oven 180°C. Peel all the vegetables, then thinly slice with a mandolin, in a food processor or by hand.

2 Blanch the vegetable slices in a pan of boiling salted water for 3–5 minutes (no longer or they will break up). Drain, reserving some of the cooking liquid, and refresh under cold running water.

3 Oil two 25cm/10in dishes. Layer the vegetables and between each layer, sprinkle over the parsley, some salt and pepper and drizzle with oil. Pour in just enough reserved liquid to cover the first layer of vegetables. Cover loosely with a double sheet of oiled greaseproof paper. Bake for 30 minutes, uncover and cook 30 minutes more until tender and golden. Garnish with parsley.

• Per serving 101 kcalories, protein 2g, carbohydrate 15g, fat 4g, saturated fat 1g, fibre 3g, added sugar trace, salt 0.35g

These pears make a fruity accompaniment for turkey and the longer they marinate, the more they pick up the spiced-wine flavours.

Roast Mulled Pears

1 medium orange, zest pared (with a vegetable peeler) and juice
300ml/½ pint red wine
2 tbsp redcurrant jelly
1 cinnamon stick, broken in half
3 whole cloves
6 just ripe pears, peeled and halved lengthways with stems intact
4 tbsp pan juices from the turkey

Takes 35 minutes, plus 3 hours marinating • Serves 10–12

1 Put the orange zest and juice in a large shallow pan with the red wine, redcurrant jelly, cinnamon and cloves. Heat gently, stirring occasionally until the jelly dissolves.

2 Put the pears in the pan. Baste with the wine juices and simmer for 10 minutes, turning occasionally. Remove from heat and leave to marinate for 3 hours or overnight.

3 When the turkey is cooked and out of the roasting tin, remove the pears from the marinade (strain the liquid and reserve for the gravy, see page 134). Put the pears in the roasting tin with 4 tablespoons of the turkey-pan juices. Turn them around in the tin to glaze with the juices and roast for 10 minutes while the turkey is resting. Serve around the turkey.

• Per serving (2 halves) 40 kcalories, protein 0.3g, carbohydrate 8g, fat 1g, saturated fat 0.1g, fibre 1g, added sugar none, salt 0.02g

The essential seasonal accompaniment to Christmas dinner, and one you can prepare up to 2 months in advance.

Cranberry Sauce

225g/8oz fresh or frozen cranberries
100g/4oz light muscovado sugar
grated zest and juice 1 small orange
6 tbsp port or red wine

Takes 15 minutes • Serves 8–10

1 Put the cranberries in a pan with the sugar, orange zest and juice and the port or red wine. Stir over a gentle heat until the sugar has dissolved, then simmer for 5–8 minutes, until the cranberries have softened and the sauce is thickened.

2 Leave to cool. Can be spooned into a rigid container and stored in the fridge for up to a week or in the freezer for up to 2 months.

• Per serving 71 kcalories, protein none, carbohydrate 15g, fat none, saturated fat none, fibre 1g, added sugar 14g, salt 0.01g

Creamy bread sauce makes Christmas dinner complete, but for a slightly less indulgent version, use créme fraîche instead of cream.

Rich Bread Sauce

700ml/1¼ pints full-fat milk
1 large onion, peeled and quartered
10 whole cloves
2 bay leaves
a few sprigs of thyme
175g/6oz fresh white breadcrumbs
6 tbsp crème fraîche or double cream
a large knob of butter
salt and freshly grated black pepper, to season
crushed mixed peppercorns, to garnish

Takes 45 minutes • Serves 10–12

1 Pour the milk into a small pan. Stud the onion quarters with the cloves and add to the pan along with the bay leaves and thyme sprigs.

2 Bring to the boil then simmer very gently for 10 minutes. Turn off the heat and leave the milk to infuse for 20 minutes.

3 Strain the milk then reheat. Stir in the breadcrumbs and simmer for 3–4 minutes, then stir in the crème fraîche or cream, butter and seasoning. Serve in a warm bowl, sprinkled with a few crushed mixed peppercorns.

• Per serving 141 kcalories, protein 4g, carbohydrate 15g, fat 8g, saturated fat 4g, fibre 1g, added sugar none, salt 0.38g

This gravy is delicious made with the juices from the Roast Mulled Pears, or you can add cinnamon and cloves to red wine instead.

Mulled Wine Gravy

5 tbsp pan juices from the turkey, skimmed of all fat
2 tbsp plain flour
marinade from the Roast Mulled Pears (see page 128, or use 200ml/7fl oz red wine mixed with a pinch of ground cinnamon and cloves)
600ml/1 pint turkey stock
salt and freshly grated black pepper, to season

Takes 15 minutes • Serves 8–10

1 Heat the pan juices in a roasting tin on the hob. Sprinkle in the flour, cook, stirring until rich golden brown in colour.
2 Gradually add the pear marinade and the stock and bring to the boil, stirring until thickened. Simmer for 5 minutes, stirring. Season and serve.

• Per serving for 8 49 kcalories, protein 4.1g, carbohydrate 4.8g, fat 0.8g, saturated fat none, fibre 0.3g, sugar 1.3g, salt 0.48g

A cheery and appetizing accompaniment to turkey
and other roast meats.

Jewelled Rice

350g/12oz long grain rice, well
rinsed and drained
2 tbsp olive oil
a small knob of butter
a pinch of saffron strands
1 tsp coriander seeds
2 tbsp pine nuts
zest of ½ orange
2 tbsp shelled pistachio nuts
seeds from 1 pomegranate
a handful each of basil, mint,
coriander leaves, chopped
salt and freshly grated black
pepper, to season
1 lemon, cut into wedges, to serve

Takes 45–55 minutes • Serves 4
(easily doubled)

1 Put the rice in a wide heavy-based pan and cover with just enough water to sit about 1cm/½ in above the grains. Season with salt, bring the water to the boil, reduce heat and simmer until all the water has been absorbed, about 10 minutes.
2 Turn off the heat, cover and leave the rice to steam for 10 minutes until it is cooked but still has bite to it.
3 In another large heavy-based pan, heat the oil and butter. Stir in the saffron, coriander seeds and pine nuts. Cook for 1 minute, then add the orange zest and pistachio nuts. Stir in the pomegranate seeds and rice. Season to taste, stir in the herbs. Serve with lemon wedges.

• Per serving 527 kcalories, protein 9g, carbohydrate 83g, fat 20g, saturated fat 5g, fibre 2g, added sugar none, salt 0.35g

You can make these a day ahead, cover and keep in the fridge,
then warm through to serve.

Baked Stuffed Red Onions

FOR THE WILD MUSHROOM STUFFING
½ × 25g pack dried porcini
mushrooms, soaked in 150ml/
¼ pint water for 20 minutes
a knob of butter
1 tbsp olive oil
1 small onion, peeled and
finely chopped
140g/5oz risotto rice
5 tbsp white wine
225ml/8fl oz chicken or vegetable
stock
50g/2oz sundried tomatoes, chopped
juice of ½ lemon

FOR THE ONIONS
8 medium-sized red onions, peeled
2 tbsp olive oil
1 tbsp balsamic vinegar
25g/1oz freshly grated parmesan

Takes about 2¼ hours • Serves 8

1 Make the stuffing. Drain and chop the mushrooms, reserving soaking liquid. Heat butter and oil in a pan, add chopped onion and fry 5 minutes. Add the rice, stir fry 2–3 minutes. Add the mushrooms, their liquid, wine and 175ml/6fl oz of the stock. Bring to boil, cover and cook until rice is just tender (add more stock if needed). Remove from heat, season, add tomatoes and lemon juice.
2 Preheat the oven to 190°C/Gas 5/fan 170°C. Cut a good slice off the top of each red onion. Put in a shallow dish in one layer and drizzle with oil and vinegar. Season. Cover tightly with foil and bake for 1 hour.
3 Carefully remove centre of each onion. Stuff and sprinkle with parmesan. Return to the oven for 15 minutes until cheese browns.

• Per serving 190 kcalories, protein 5g, carbohydrate 27g, fat 7g, saturated fat 2g, fibre 2g, added sugar none, salt 0.85g

This terrine is a cinch to make and perfect served as a starter with crisp French toast and tomato chutney.

Pork and Pistachio Terrine

12–18 rashers smoked streaky bacon
3 large garlic cloves, sliced
25g/1oz butter
800g/1lb 12oz minced pork
50g/2oz pistachio nuts
1 tsp salt
3 tbsp fresh thyme leaves
25g/1oz dried cranberries
3 tbsp brandy
1 large egg, beaten
200g/7oz fresh chicken livers, chopped
freshly ground black pepper, to season

Takes 1 hour 35 minutes • Serves 10 as a starter

1 Preheat the oven to 180°C/Gas 4/fan oven 160°C. Line a 900g/2lb loaf tin with 6–12 rashers of bacon (depending on shape of tin), slightly overlapping them and letting the excess hang over the top of the tin.

2 Fry the garlic in the butter for a minute, cool briefly, then mix with the remaining ingredients except the livers. Season generously with black pepper. Press half the mince mixture into the tin, then lay the livers on top. Cover with the remaining mince mixture, then top with the remaining 6 bacon rashers, cutting them in half for a neat fit if necessary. Fold over the overhanging bacon.

3 Bake for 1 hour 15 minutes. Pour off most of the liquid, cover with foil and put a weight on top of the terrine as it cools to compact the texture. Cool then chill.

• Per serving 294 kcalories, protein 25g, carbohydrate 3g, fat 19g, saturated fat 7g, fibre none, sugar 2g, salt 1.5g

Light, colourful and seasonal, this salad
is an ideal starter for two.

Christmas Salad with Goats' Cheese

100g/4oz goats' cheese (round with a rind)
1 ripe pear
a handful of pecan nuts or other nuts, roughly broken
80g bag mixed watercress and spinach
crusty bread, to serve
oil, for brushing

FOR THE DRESSING
1 tbsp cranberry sauce
1 tbsp olive oil
1 tbsp lemon juice

Takes 20–30 minutes •
Serves 2 as a starter

1 Preheat the grill to high and line the grill rack with foil. Halve the cheese to make two discs. Halve and core the pear, cut each half into slices and arrange in two piles on the foil.
2 Lightly brush the pears with oil then top each pile with a cheese disc (cut side up) and grill for a few minutes until lightly golden and bubbling. Scatter with the nuts and grill for a minute or so more.
3 To make the dressing, whisk the cranberry sauce with the oil and lemon juice and season. Arrange salad leaves on two plates. Put the pears and cheese on top. Spoon over the dressing, scatter over any stray nuts and eat right away with crusty bread while the cheese is still deliciously runny.

• Per serving 327 kcalories, protein 13g, carbohydrate 12g, fat 26g, saturated fat 10g, fibre 3g, added sugar 2g, salt 0.99g

Served with cucumber pickle, horseradish cream and warm bread, this platter makes a simple lunch or a substantial starter.

Platter of Arbroath Smokies

3 pairs Arbroath smokies, skinned and boned, chunks of flesh removed
2 large cucumbers, thinly sliced
1 small onion, peeled and thinly sliced into wedges
50g/2oz golden caster sugar
6 tbsp white wine vinegar
2 tbsp mustard seeds, optional
4 tbsp creamed horseradish
500ml tub crème fraîche
1 large bunch parsley, chopped
4 large lemons, cut into wedges
warm soda bread, to serve

Takes about 1¼ hours, including soaking and chilling • Serves 8 as a starter

1 Put the chunks of smokies on a large platter, cover with cling film and chill.
2 Layer the cucumber slices with the onion in a colander, sprinkling with a little salt. Set aside for 1 hour. Rinse under the cold tap to remove excess salt. Pat the cucumber and onion dry on kitchen paper. Stir the sugar in a bowl with 4 tablespoons of boiling water. When dissolved, add vinegar and the cucumber mixture. Season with pepper, stir in the mustard seeds (if using). Cover, chill for 1 hour or overnight.
3 To serve, remove platter from the fridge and let come to room temperature. Mix the horseradish and crème fraîche. Stir the parsley into the cucumber pickle. Put the lemon wedges on the platter.

• Per serving 336 kcalories, protein 18g, carbohydrate 15g, fat 23g, saturated fat 11g, fibre 1g, added sugar 7g, salt 1.73g

A simple blended soup that can be made ahead of time and frozen or served up straightaway with sesame breadsticks or fresh bread.

Frothy Cannellini Soup

3 tbsp olive oil
1 large onion, finely chopped
2 garlic cloves, crushed
1 medium leek, thinly sliced
3 sticks celery, finely chopped
2 × 400g cans cannellini beans, drained and rinsed
1.7 litres/3 pints vegetable stock
1 bay leaf
142ml carton double cream
150g pot fresh green pesto from the chiller cabinet
salt and freshly ground black pepper, to season
125g pack (around 16) sesame bread sticks, to serve (optional)

Takes 30 minutes •
Serves 8 as a starter

1 Heat the oil in a large pan and tip in the onion, garlic, leek and celery. Cover and sweat the vegetables over a low heat for 8–10 minutes until softened. Add the beans, stock and bay leaf, then season and bring to the boil. Reduce the heat, then simmer, covered, for 20–25 minutes until the vegetables are completely softened. Allow to cool slightly.

2 Whiz with a stick blender until smooth, pour in the cream and reheat. The soup can be chilled or frozen at this point.

3 Before serving, add half the pesto and whiz again for just a few seconds until the soup is flecked with basil. Season to taste. Ladle the soup into 8 cappuccino cups or bowls and spoon a dollop of the remaining pesto into each serving.

• Per serving 345 kcalories, protein 13g, carbohydrate 22g, fat 23g, saturated fat 8g, fibre 5g, added sugar none, salt 1.62g

Cure the salmon at least 3 days ahead then it can sit in the fridge for up to a week and be used just like smoked salmon.

Dazzling Beetroot-Cured Salmon

2 skin-on salmon fillets (about
1.3 kg/3lb), pin bones removed
1 frisée, or oak leaf lettuce
4 beetroot, cooked, peeled, diced
2 shallots, peeled, finely chopped

FOR THE CURE
225g/8oz caster sugar
140g/5oz sea salt flakes
85g/3oz fresh horseradish, peeled
and finely grated, or from a jar
3 raw beetroot, coarsely grated
1 bunch dill, chopped

FOR THE DRESSING
200ml tub crème fraîche
juice of 1 lemon
2 tbsp freshly grated horseradish
handful dill fronds, roughly chopped

Takes 30 minutes, plus 3 days curing •
Serves 8–12 as a starter

1 Mix all the cure ingredients together. Stretch two large sheets of cling film over a work surface and spoon over some of the cure. Lay one of the salmon fillets, skin side down, on it. Pack over most of the cure. Sandwich with remaining fillet, skin side up.
2 Top with remaining cure, securely wrap fillets together with cling film. Place in a container with sides, put a smaller tray on top. Weigh down with two tins. Chill for 3 days to 1 week. Every day, pour off any liquid, turn the salmon and re-apply weights.
3 To serve, unwrap the salmon, brush off the marinade. Thinly slice the fish. Mix dressing ingredients together, season. Toss the salad ingredients and serve a handful with a few salmon slices and a drizzle of dressing.

• Per serving for 12 306 kcalories, protein 23g, carbohydrate 7g, fat 21g, saturated fat 7g, fibre 1g, added sugar 4g, salt 2.27g

Trout makes a sensational variation on the popular combination
of smoked salmon with blinis.

Smoked Trout and Dill Blinis

225g/8oz smoked trout fillets
(usually vacuum-packed)
100ml/3½fl oz crème fraîche
1 tbsp chopped fresh dill, plus extra,
roughly chopped, to garnish
2 tsp lemon juice
6 ready-made large blinis or
18 small ones
1 small jar black herring roe
salt and freshly ground black
pepper, to season

Takes about 15 minutes • Serves 6

1 Break the smoked trout into bite-sized
pieces (the easiest way is to use your hands).
Mix together the crème fraîche, chopped dill
and lemon juice in a small bowl, then season
with salt and pepper.
2 Just before serving, toast the blinis on each
side. Put one on each plate (or 3 if using
small ones) and top with a spoonful of the
crème-fraîche mixture, then some trout
pieces, then a spoonful of the herring roe.
3 Garnish with the roughly chopped dill and
serve immediately.

• Per serving 165 kcalories, protein 10g, carbohydrate
11g, fat 9g, saturated fat 5g, fibre trace, added sugar
1g, salt 0.3g

A prepare-ahead recipe suitable for a small gathering.
Good served with rice and garnished with chilli and spring onion.

Hot Salmon Parcel

1.8kg/4lb salmon, filleted and cut in half lengthways
2 tbsp lime juice
2 tbsp clear honey
2 tbsp soy sauce

FOR THE STUFFING
1 bunch spring onions, shredded
1 small thin fresh red chilli, halved lengthways, seeded, cut in slivers
a large knob of fresh root ginger (7.5cm/3in long), peeled, in slivers
2 plump garlic cloves, crushed
2 tbsp sunflower oil, for frying
50g/2oz creamed coconut from a block, chopped or crumbled
400g/14oz raw peeled large prawns

1 red chilli, seeded, cut into thin strips
1–2 spring onions, shredded

Takes about 1¼ hours • Serves 4

1 Preheat oven to 240°C/Gas 9/fan oven 220°C. Stir fry onions, chilli, ginger and garlic for stuffing, in oil, 3–4 minutes. Stir in coconut until melted. Add prawns, fry 2–3 minutes. Tip into a bowl, season, cool.
2 Score salmon skin of one fillet in criss-cross diagonal lines. Lay out a sheet of parchment (size of base of roasting tin), one long side facing you. Cut four 30cm/12in pieces of string, lay at equal intervals on paper. Put unscored fillet, skin side down, across string.
3 Spread stuffing over fillet. Top with scored fillet, skin side up. Tie with string. Put empty roasting tin in oven. Lay salmon on the paper in hot roasting tin. Roast 15–20 minutes. Heat lime juice, honey, soy sauce in pan. Transfer salmon to platter, splash over sauce. Rest 5 minutes. Serve with sauce.

• Per serving 736 kcalories, protein 76g, carbohydrate 6g, fat 46g, saturated fat 14g, fibre 2g, added sugar 3g, salt 0.95g

This crunchy, spicy ham makes a mouth-watering centrepiece and looks enticing dressed with oranges, bay leaves and juniper berries.

Festive Spiced Ham

2.7-3.6kg/6-8lb smoked or unsmoked boned gammon
1 onion and 1 orange, halved and studded with 12 cloves
1 cinnamon stick, broken in half
4 bay leaves, plus extra to garnish
6 juniper berries, coarsely bruised, plus extra left whole, to garnish
500ml can sweet cider
2 oranges, quartered
Cumberland sauce, to serve

FOR THE GLAZE
6 tbsp clear honey
zest of 1 orange and 2 tbsp juice

FOR THE TOPPING
50g/2oz fresh white breadcrumbs
a large knob of butter, softened
a handful parsley leaves, chopped

Takes 20 minutes, plus about 3½ hours cooking • Serves 8–12 (with leftovers)

1 Put gammon in large pan with onion and orange halves, cinnamon, bay, juniper and cider. Top up with water. Bring to boil, cover, simmer (allow 20 minutes per 450g/1lb, plus 20 minutes). Keep topped up with water.
2 Preheat oven to 220°C/Gas 7/fan oven 200°C. Remove gammon, cool slightly. Cut away skin, leaving layer of fat. Transfer to roasting tin with 4 tablespoons cooking liquid and orange quarters. Mix honey, orange juice and zest. Brush some over ham and oranges. Bake 15 minutes. Brush with more glaze, bake 15 minutes, basting two or three times until golden and starting to char.
3 Make topping. Spread crumbs on baking sheet. Put in oven for 8–10 minutes, stirring often, until golden. Brush ham with glaze, mix warm crumbs with butter and parsley and press on ham. Serve with accompaniments.

• Per serving for 8 536 kcalories, protein 52.7g, carbohydrate 17.2g, fat 28.9g, saturated fat 11.3g, fibre 0.8g, sugar 12.5g, salt 6.79g

Beef Wellington is a classic dinner dish – in this recipe the meat is kept deliciously moist by a layer of chopped mushrooms.

Beef Wellington

1 tbsp olive oil
1.15kg/2½lb thick beef fillet, tied with string to keep its shape
1 shallot, peeled and finely chopped
100g/4oz chestnut mushrooms, finely chopped
a generous knob of butter
3 tbsp chopped fresh parsley
500g packet puff pastry, thawed if frozen
beaten egg, to glaze
2 tsp plain flour
600ml/1 pint good-quality stock, such as chicken or lamb
6 tbsp red wine
1–2 tbsp Dijon mustard
watercress and fresh herbs such as thyme and parsley, to garnish

Takes 1 hour 20–1 hour 35 minutes • Serves 6

1 Preheat oven to 220°C/Gas 7/fan oven 200°C. Heat oil in frying pan to high, brown beef. Roast in tin 15 minutes for rare, 20 for medium rare, 25–30 for medium-well done.
2 Fry shallot and mushrooms in butter until no juices remain. Remove, add parsley, season, cool. Transfer beef (keep juices) to platter lined with kitchen paper. Cool, remove string. Roll pastry so will wrap around beef. Keep trimmings. Spread mushroom mix down centre. Top with beef. Brush pastry edges with egg, bring the ends then sides over beef, seal. Put on baking sheet, join underneath. Brush with egg, decorate with pastry shapes made from trimmings. Bake 35–40 minutes until golden.
3 Heat juices in roasting tin, add flour. Stir until browned. Add stock and wine, reduce to thicken. Stir in mustard. Garnish.

• Per serving for 6 679 kcalories, protein 51.6g, carbohydrate 33.6g, fat 37.4g, saturated fat 14.5g, fibre 0.8g, sugar 1.8g, salt 1.66g

The sauce can be made up to 30 minutes ahead, then reheated gently before being put in a bowl to serve.

Roast Guinea Fowl with Mushroom Sauce

5 shallots, 3 peeled, 2 finely chopped
3 × 1.5kg/3lb 5oz guinea fowl
few sprigs fresh thyme
2 tbsp olive oil
25g/1oz dried mushrooms, such as porcini or morel
1 tsp vegetable bouillon or ½ stock cube
300g/10oz chestnut mushrooms, sliced
125ml/4fl oz Pineau or sherry
1 tbsp wholegrain mustard
3 rounded tbsp crème fraîche
salt and freshly ground black pepper, to season

Takes about 2 hours • Serves 8

1 Preheat the oven to 190°C/Gas 5/fan oven 170°C. Put one shallot inside each bird with thyme and seasoning. Put in a roasting tin, drizzle with oil, season, roast for 1¼–1½ hours until golden.

2 Meanwhile, put the dried mushrooms and stock in a measuring jug, pour in boiling water to 250ml/9fl oz. Leave 30 minutes. Remove cooked bird from the oven, transfer to a warm serving plate. Cover tightly with double layer of foil, let rest 30 minutes. Drain off all but 2 tablespoons of fat from the pan.

3 Drain dried mushrooms, reserve the liquid, then chop. Reheat pan juices, add chopped shallots and all mushrooms. Fry quickly to soften, stir in the Pineau, mushroom liquid and mustard. Boil rapidly to reduce, about 5 minutes. Stir in the crème fraîche.

• Per serving 591 kcalories, protein 76g, carbohydrate 3g, fat 28g, saturated fat 10g, fibre 1g, sugar 2g, salt 0.84g

The ham is cooked in the oven, which entails half baking, half steaming so it stays moist.

Christmas Ham with Sticky Ginger Glaze

1 uncooked ham (about 5kg/11lb), soaked according to instructions
1 large onion, peeled, thickly sliced
5cm/2in piece fresh ginger, sliced
1 small bunch fresh thyme
5 cloves
sprigs of bay leaves, to garnish

FOR THE GLAZE
175g/6oz light muscovado sugar
2.5cm/1in piece fresh ginger, peeled and sliced
10 kumquats, thickly sliced, pips discarded, plus extra, halved
3 pieces preserved stem ginger in syrup, cut into small strips
1 tsp ground ginger
10–15 cloves

Takes about 5 hours, including 4½ hours total in oven, plus soaking and resting times • Serves 8–10 (with lots of leftovers)

1 Preheat oven to 180°C/Gas 4/fan oven 160°C. Weigh ham, calculate cooking time (25 minutes per 500g/1lb 2oz). Scatter onion, ginger, thyme, cloves into roasting tin. Add ham, then water to 3–5cm/1¼–2in deep. Cover all with tent of thick foil. Bake 1½ hours then reduce heat to 160°C/Gas 3/fan oven 140°C. Remove, rest 30 minutes.
2 Dissolve sugar in 100ml/3½fl oz water. Add ginger, simmer. Add kumquats for 3 minutes. Remove and reserve kumquats, discard ginger, add stem ginger. Reduce by half.
3 Unwrap ham, transfer to oiled foil-lined tin. Cut off skin, score fat. Raise oven to 220°C/Gas 7/fan oven 200°C. Rub ground ginger over ham, brush on most of glaze. Scatter over kumquat slices, stud some with cloves. Drizzle over remaining glaze. Roast 20 minutes. Garnish with kumquats and bay.

• Per serving for 8 379 kcalories, protein 40g, carbohydrate 8g, fat 21g, saturated fat 8g, fibre none, added sugar 6g, salt 5.14g

Goose is a rich alternative to turkey on Christmas Day, but it doesn't provide as much meat, so don't scrimp on the size or quantity.

Christmas Roast Goose

4.5kg/10lb trussed and oven-ready fresh goose with giblets
1 quantity Apricot and Coriander Stuffing (see page 100)
sea or rock salt, for sprinkling
fresh mint, parsley and bay leaves, to garnish

FOR THE GIBLET STOCK
goose giblets (excluding fat, liver)
½ large onion, peeled and sliced
pared zest 1 large orange
small handful of parsley stalks
2 bay leaves, torn
about 6 black peppercorns

FOR THE GRAVY
2 tbsp plain flour
600ml/1pint of the giblet stock
juice of 1 orange and 4–6 tbsp port
1 tbsp redcurrant jelly

Takes about 4½ hours • Serves 6–8

1 Simmer giblets in 1.7 litres/3 pints water and stock ingredients for 1½–2 hours. Strain. Chill.
2 Preheat oven to 190°C/Gas 5/fan oven 170°C. Spoon stuffing into goose's body cavity. Put in roasting tin, prick breast several times with a fork, sprinkle with salt. Cover with a loose tent of thick foil. Roast for 1½ hours. Open the foil, remove as much fat as possible from tin. Re-cover goose, roast 1 hour. Open foil to expose breast only, roast 30 minutes more. Test if cooked (see page 88). Transfer goose to warm platter. Cover loosely with foil. Rest 30 minutes.
3 For gravy, leave 2 tablespoons of fat in roasting tin. Put tin on hob and reheat. Add flour, stirring until well browned. Pour in stock gradually, simmer 5 minutes. Add remaining gravy ingredients, simmer to thicken. Serve with roasted apples and onions and a herb garnish.

• Per serving for 6 1072 kcalories, protein 94.9g, carbohydrate 25.7g, fat 65.1g, saturated fat 19.5g, fibre 3.1g, sugar 11.1g, salt 2.23g

If you want to get ahead, the meat and sauce for this seasonal pie can be made 2 days in advance.

Venison Pie

2kg/4lb 8oz venison steak, cut into 2.5cm/1in cubes
300ml/½ pint red wine
8 tbsp olive oil
3 bay leaves
5 juniper berries, lightly crushed
10 fresh thyme sprigs
24 shallots, peeled but left whole
2 tbsp plain flour
500ml/18fl oz vegetable stock
1 tbsp Dijon mustard
500g/1lb 2oz large cap chestnut mushrooms, quartered
2 tbsp redcurrant jelly
500g/1lb 2oz ready-to-roll puff pastry, thawed if frozen, rolled and scored in criss-cross pattern
beaten egg, for brushing

Takes 45 minutes, plus overnight marinating • Serves 12

1 Marinate venison in wine, 3 tablespoons oil, bay, juniper and 5 thyme sprigs overnight.
2 Preheat oven to 160°C/Gas 3/fan oven 140°C. Fry shallots in 2 tablespoons oil for 5 minutes. Drain meat (reserve marinade). Brown venison in batches in 2 tablespoons hot oil in large pan. Put in casserole with shallots. Add flour to last meat batch, brown 2–3 minutes. Stir into casserole with marinade, stock, mustard. Season. Bring to boil. Cover, cook in oven 1½ hours. Fry mushrooms in oil, stir into meat with redcurrant jelly and remaining thyme. Tip into 2.5 litre/4½ pint pie dish. Chill.
3 Preheat oven to 200°C/Gas 6/fan oven 180°C. Cover meat with pastry, flute edges, brush with egg, make cross in centre. Bake 20–25 minutes, reduce oven to 160°C/Gas 3/fan oven 140°C. Bake 1 hour.

• Per serving 482 kcalories, protein 43g, carbohydrate 22g, fat 22g, saturated fat 3g, fibre 1g, added sugar 2g, salt 0.68g

Rack of lamb is a great choice for two people – and when flavoured with spices is an ideal Christmassy treat.

Moroccan Spiced Rack of Lamb

5 tbsp olive oil
1–1½ tbsp harissa paste
¼ tsp each turmeric, paprika, ground coriander and cumin
20g pack fresh flat-leaf parsley, chopped
juice of ½ small lemon
1 rack of lamb (6–8 cutlets)
2 carrots, peeled and cut into chunks
100g/4oz couscous
150ml/¼ pint hot vegetable stock
juice of 1 satsuma
¼ tsp ground allspice
½ × 20g pack fresh mint, chopped
½ red onion, peeled, finely chopped
Greek yoghurt and 50g/2oz flaked almonds, toasted, to serve

Takes 40–45 minutes • Serves 2

1 Preheat the oven to 220°C/Gas 7/fan oven 200°C. Mix 2 tablespoons of the oil with the harissa, turmeric, paprika, coriander, cumin, half the parsley, lemon juice and a pinch of salt. Season lamb, spread with spice mix then roast for 15–20 minutes for rare-medium, 25 minutes for well done.
2 Meanwhile, toss carrots in a small roasting tin, with a pinch of salt and 1 tablespoon of the oil. Roast for 15 minutes. Meanwhile, tip couscous into bowl, pour over hot stock and let stand for 5 minutes. Stir and cool. Stir in remaining oil and parsley, satsuma juice, allspice, mint, onion, carrots and season.
3 Rest lamb for 5 minutes. Slice in half for 3–4 cutlets each, then halve again. Serve with yoghurt and couscous with almonds.

• Per serving 888 kcalories, protein 34g, carbohydrate 40g, fat 67g, saturated fat 18g, fibre 5g, added sugar none, salt 1.22g

A delicious, hearty pie, perfect served with leftovers
as part of a Boxing Day buffet.

Christmas Pie

1 onion, peeled and finely chopped

a knob of butter

2 tbsp olive oil

500g/1lb 2oz sausagemeat

grated zest 1 lemon

100g/4oz fresh white breadcrumbs

85g/3oz ready-to-eat dried apricots, chopped

50g/2oz chestnuts, canned or vacuum-packed, chopped

2 tsp chopped fresh or 1 tsp dried thyme

100g/4oz cranberries, fresh or frozen (thawed)

500g/1lb 2oz boneless, skinless chicken breasts, each cut into 3 lengthways fillets and seasoned

500g ready-rolled shortcrust pastry

beaten egg, to glaze

Takes 1¾ hours • Serves 10–12

1 Preheat oven to 190°C/ Gas 5/fan oven 170°C. Fry the onion in butter and half the oil for 5 minutes until soft. Cool. Mix the sausagemeat, lemon zest, breadcrumbs, apricots, chestnuts and thyme in a bowl, add the onion and cranberries. Season. Heat rest of oil in frying pan, brown the chicken.

2 Roll out two-thirds of the pastry and line a 20–23cm/8–9in springform or deep loose-based tart tin. Press in half the sausage mix. Add chicken pieces in one layer, cover with remaining sausage. Roll out remaining pastry for lid. Brush edges with egg, cover with lid, seal and trim edges. Brush top with egg. Decorate with holly-leaf shapes and berries made from pastry trimmings. Glaze again.

3 Bake for 50–60 minutes. Cool in tin for 15 minutes. Remove and cool.

• Per serving 488 kcalories, protein 23g, carbohydrate 39g, fat 28g, saturated fat 12g, fibre 2g, added sugar none, salt 1.4g

Duck legs roasted French-style in goose fat are mouth-wateringly tender. Cook them a month ahead then roast them briefly on the day.

Duck with Madeira Gravy

FOR THE DUCK
25g/1oz sea salt flakes
2 tsp crushed black peppercorns
4 fresh bay leaves
1 tsp fresh thyme leaves, plus 2–4 sprigs
2 large or 4 small duck legs (550g/1lb 4oz total weight)
340g can goose fat
about 300ml/½ pint groundnut oil

FOR THE MADEIRA GRAVY
2 shallots, peeled, finely chopped
generous knob of butter, melted
1 tsp plain flour
300g tub fresh chicken stock
2 tbsp Madeira

Takes 3–3½ hours, plus overnight salting • Serves 2
Moderately easy

1 Mix salt, pepper, herbs (except thyme sprigs) in bowl. Add duck, rub in mix. Cover, chill overnight. Wipe off salt, place duck in one tight layer in pan. Add the bay leaves from bowl, pour over goose fat. Cover with groundnut oil. Cook over lowest heat, 2½ hours, so fat barely bubbles. Transfer duck to bowl, strain in fat to submerge fully.
2 Fry shallots for gravy in the melted butter 6–8 minutes until golden. Add flour, stir until browned. Whisk in stock until slightly thickened. Add Madeira, cook 2 minutes. Strain into bowl. (Can chill up to 2 days.)
3 Preheat oven to 200°C/Gas 6/fan oven 180°C. Remove duck, wipe off excess fat. Put on wire rack in roasting tin, add thyme sprigs. Roast 40 minutes until golden. Reheat gravy. Serve with red cabbage, shallots and sugar snap peas.

• Per serving 890 kcalories, protein 48g, carbohydrate 27g, fat 64g, saturated fat 18g, fibre 6g, added sugar 3g, salt 2.17g

This flamboyant filo-pastry pie is a great vegetarian option for Christmas Day. Serve with yoghurt and lemon wedges.

Moroccan Spiced Pie

2 tsp each coriander and cumin seeds, dry fried until brown, coarsely ground
1 tsp paprika, plus extra for dusting
½ tsp ground cinnamon
6 tbsp olive oil
900g/2lb squash, peeled and cut into small chunks (about 2cm/¾in)
12 shallots, peeled, quartered
4cm/1½in piece root ginger, finely chopped
140g/5oz whole blanched almonds
140g/5oz shelled pistachios
75g pack dried cranberries
6 tbsp clear honey
225g pack fresh spinach
8 large sheets filo pastry
12oz houmous, mixed with 4 tbsp chopped fresh coriander
100g/4oz butter, melted

Takes 1¾–2 hours • Serves 6

1 Preheat oven to 200°C/Gas 6/fan oven 180°C. Mix seeds, paprika, cinnamon, ½ tsp salt, 4 tablespoons oil. Add squash, toss. Roast 20 minutes. Fry shallots in remaining oil. Stir in ginger and 100g/4oz each almonds and pistachios to brown. Add cranberries, 2 tablespoons honey, and spinach to wilt. Stir into roasted squash.
2 Put a buttered loose-bottomed 28cm/11in tin on baking sheet. Lay one filo sheet over half the tin to hang well over edge. Lay another sheet opposite, overlap in centre. Brush with butter. Lay two more sheets in opposite direction, butter, then lay two more.
3 Pile half squash mixture in centre. Spread over houmous then more squash. Gather filo into centre. Brush with butter. Bake 30–35 minutes. Reheat butter in pan, tip in remaining nuts and fry. Add rest of honey, pour over pie.

• Per serving for 6 865 kcalories, protein 19.8g, carbohydrate 66.7g, fat 59.6g, saturated fat 14g, fibre 7g, sugar 33.5g, salt 2.16g

A rustic, savoury vegetarian pie, flavoured with grilled artichokes, wild mushrooms and finished with soured cream.

Artichoke and Wild Mushroom Pie

3 tbsp olive oil
2 large onions, peeled, finely sliced
300g/10oz grilled artichoke hearts (from the deli, or a jar), halved
300g/10oz mixed mushrooms (wild or cultivated), halved if large
1 garlic clove, crushed
1 tsp fresh thyme leaves
500g pack ready-rolled shortcrust pastry
1 egg, a pinch of salt and 1 tbsp water, beaten together to glaze
large handful flat-leaf parsley leaves, very roughly chopped
142ml carton soured cream, to serve
salt and freshly ground black pepper, to season

Takes 1 hour • Serves 6

1 Preheat the oven to 200°C/ Gas 6/fan oven 180°C. Heat half the oil in a frying pan, then gently fry the onions for 12–15 minutes until softened and lightly browned. Tip them into a bowl, mix with the artichoke hearts, season, set aside. Heat remaining oil in the same pan, stir fry the mushrooms for 2–3 minutes until soft. Add garlic and thyme, cook 1 more minute. Season, let cool.
2 On a floured surface, roll out the pastry to a rough 40cm/16in circle. Drape over a large baking sheet. Pile on onions and artichokes and spread out evenly, leaving a 10cm/4in border at the edge. Top with mushrooms.
3 Bring pastry edges over the filling. Brush exposed edge with the egg glaze. Bake for 20–25 minutes until crisp and golden. Serve with soured cream, sprinkled with parsley.

• Per serving 560 kcalories, protein 7g, carbohydrate 44g, fat 41g, saturated fat 14g, fibre 4g, added sugar none, salt 1.55g

A sensational vegetarian main course that looks impressive
on any celebratory dinner table.

Creamy Risotto Layer Cake

300g/10oz shallots, peeled, half
chopped, the rest thinly sliced
4 tbsp olive oil
2 garlic cloves, crushed
500g pack risotto rice
200ml/7fl oz white wine
1.2–1.4 litres/2–2½ pints hot vegetable
stock
about 50g/2oz butter
100g/4oz vegetarian-style parmesan,
finely grated
1 large butternut squash (about
1.2kg/2½lb unprepped weight),
peeled and cut into small cubes
200g/7oz chestnuts, roughly chopped
100g pack pine nuts, toasted
1 small bunch sage, chopped
2 sprigs rosemary, finely chopped
about 10 large outside green savoy
cabbage leaves, blanched, drained
250g tub mascarpone

Takes just over 2 hours, plus overnight
chilling • Serves 8–10

1 Fry chopped shallots in 2 tablespoons oil.
Add garlic, stir in rice. Fry, stir in wine. When
absorbed, ladle in stock gradually. Add knob
of butter and 25g/1oz parmesan. Season.
Cool. Preheat oven to 200°C/Gas 6/fan oven
180°C. Toss squash with 1 tablespoon oil,
roast 30 minutes until golden. Fry sliced
shallots in butter and 1 tablespoon oil for 15
minutes. Stir in chestnuts, pine nuts, herbs.
Season, cook 2 minutes. Mix with squash.
2 Line buttered 23cm/9in cake tin with most
of cabbage, overlap and overhang. Mix rest
of parmesan and mascarpone, season. Pile
in half risotto, then squash, mascarpone, then
remaining risotto. Fold over cabbage, 'seal'
with remaining leaves. Cover with cling film,
weight down, chill overnight.
3 Cover cake with buttered foil. Reheat 30
minutes at 180°C/ Gas 4/fan oven 160°C.

• Per serving 722 kcalories, protein 18g, carbohydrate
75g, fat 40g, saturated fat 17g, fibre 6g, sugar 13g,
salt 1.53g

The classic end to the traditional Christmas dinner.
Serve with brandy butter or sauce.

Classic Christmas Pudding

1 whole nutmeg (you'll use ¾ of it)
2 large Bramley cooking apples,
peeled, cored and chopped
50g/2oz blanched almonds,
chopped
200g box candied peel (in large
pieces), chopped
1kg/2lb 4oz raisins
140g/5oz plain flour
100g/4oz soft fresh breadcrumbs
100g/4oz light muscovado sugar
3 large eggs
2 tbsp brandy or cognac, plus extra
for serving
250g packet firm butter, plus extra
for greasing

Takes 45–55 minutes, plus 9 hours
cooking • Makes two 1.2 litre/2 pint
puddings (each serves 8)

1 Grate three-quarters of the nutmeg. Mix all the pudding ingredients, except the butter, in a large bowl. Holding the butter in its wrapper, grate a quarter of it into the bowl. Stir. Repeat until all the butter is grated, then stir for 3–4 minutes.

2 Generously butter two 1.2 litre/2 pint bowls and line the bases. Pack in the pudding mixture. Cover tightly and steam for 8 hours, topping up with water as necessary. Remove from the pans. Cool overnight. Re-wrap. Store in a cool, dry place until Christmas (can be made about 2 months ahead).

3 To serve, boil each pudding for 1 hour. Unwrap and turn out. Warm 3–4 tablespoons of brandy in a small pan, pour over the pudding and set light to it.

• Per serving 550 kcalories, protein 5g, carbohydrate 77g, fat 25g, saturated fat 6g, fibre 2g, added sugar 16g, salt 0.92g

This lighter version of a traditional Christmas pudding,
can be made 2 days ahead then re-steamed for 1½ hours on the day.

Tropical Fruit Pudding with Maple Syrup

225g/8oz dark raisins
3 tbsp dark rum
50g/2oz light muscovado sugar
3 tbsp maple syrup
85g/3oz butter, softened
375g/13oz tropical dried fruit
50g/2oz mixed roasted walnuts,
whole blanched hazelnuts, almonds
50g/2oz each whole blanched hazelnuts, almonds, roasted walnut halves
175g/6oz butter, softened
50g/2oz light muscovado sugar
85g/3oz dark muscovado sugar
3 tbsp maple syrup, plus extra
3 eggs
grated zest and juice 1 mandarin
50g/2oz roasted, chopped hazelnuts
175g/6oz self-raising flour
50g/2oz ground almonds
1 tsp ground cinnamon
holly and icing sugar, to decorate

Takes about 1 hour, plus 3 hours cooking
• Serves 10–12

1 Soak raisins in the rum. Butter a 2–2.25 litre/3½–4 pint pudding basin. Beat sugar, maple syrup and butter. Put a large handful of tropical fruits and the mixed nuts in the basin. Spread maple butter on top.
2 Chop most of the nuts (leave a few whole), and remaining tropical fruits. Beat butter, sugars and maple syrup until fluffy. Add eggs, one at a time, beating well. Fold in mandarin zest and chopped hazelnuts, then the flour a third at a time with ground almonds and cinnamon. Fold in nuts, tropical fruits, raisins, rum and 2 tablespoons of mandarin juice. Spoon into basin. Level the top, cover, steam for 3 hours.
3 Remove from pan, leave 5 minutes. Invert pudding on to plate. Drizzle with extra syrup, add holly and dust with icing sugar.

• Per serving 812 kcalories, protein 11g, carbohydrate 81g, fat 50g, saturated fat 23g, fibre 5g, added sugar 26g, salt 0.88g

This is an amazingly quick, last-minute recipe. Or it can be made up to a month ahead, then reheated in the microwave for 10 minutes.

Last-Minute Christmas Pudding

300g/10oz good-quality mincemeat
140g/5oz fine-shred orange marmalade
225g/8oz molasses cane sugar
4 tbsp black treacle
3 eggs, beaten
4 tbsp whisky
100g/4oz butter, frozen and coarsely grated
225g/8oz self-raising flour
brandy butter or cream, to serve

Takes 35 minutes • Serves 6–8

1 Butter and line the base of a 1.5-litre/2¾-pint pudding basin with greaseproof paper. In a large bowl, stir the ingredients together, adding them one at a time in the order they are listed, until everything is completely mixed.
2 Tip the pudding mix into the basin and cover with a circle of greaseproof paper. Place the pudding basin on a plate and microwave on Medium for 20–25 minutes until cooked and an inserted skewer comes out clean. Leave to stand for 5 minutes, then turn out and serve with brandy butter or cream.

• Per serving for 6 634 kcalories, protein 7g, carbohydrate 108g, fat 20g, saturated fat 11g, fibre 2g, added sugar 73g, salt 1g

A deliciously moist alternative to the traditional pudding made by combining two favourite bakes – sticky toffee pudding and carrot cake.

Blitz-and-Bake Sticky Toffee Pud

225g/8oz ready-to-eat stoned dates
100g/4oz walnuts
1 carrot, peeled and coarsely grated
in the food processor
1 dessert apple (Cox's are good)
peeled, cored and coarsely
grated in the food processor
2 tbsp golden syrup
4 tbsp brandy
100g/4oz cold butter, cut into cubes
2 eggs, beaten
140g/5oz golden caster sugar
175g/6oz self-raising flour
1 tsp bicarbonate of soda

FOR THE PRALINE AND TOFFEE SAUCE
175g/6oz golden caster sugar
25g/1oz walnuts, roughly chopped
100g/4oz butter
6 tbsp double cream

Takes 1 hour 50 minutes • Serves 6–8

1 Preheat oven to 160°C/Gas 3/fan oven 140°C. Butter and line base of 1.5-litre/2¾-pint pudding basin. Roughly chop the dates in a food processor. Add walnuts, carrot, apple, golden syrup and brandy. Pulse to chop coarsely. Tip in the butter, eggs and sugar. Pulse to combine. Add the flour and bicarbonate, pulse. Spoon into basin. Bake for 1 hour 20 minutes–1 hour 30 minutes.
2 Cook the sugar for the praline in a frying pan, over a medium heat until golden. Add the walnuts to coat, then lift out with a slotted spoon on to a paper-lined tray. Let harden. Add the butter and cream to the caramel pan, bring to a simmer, stir.
3 Break praline into shards. Turn out the pudding, decorate with some sauce and praline. Serve with remaining sauce.

• Per serving for 8 703 kcalories, protein 7g, carbohydrate 81g, fat 39g, saturated fat 18g, fibre 3g, added sugar 44g, salt 1g

This pudding is great if you want a dessert that looks like Christmas pud, but is altogether different.

Iced Berry Pud

284ml carton double cream
500g carton good-quality ready-made custard
100g/4oz golden caster sugar
100ml/3½fl oz dark rum, plus 1 tbsp extra
170g packet dried berries and cherries (or same weight mix of dried cranberries, cherries, blueberries and raisins)
sprigs of sugar-frosted bay leaves and little bunches of sugar-frosted red and green grapes, to decorate

Takes 20–30 minutes, plus 2½ hours chilling and cooling and overnight freezing • Serves 6–8

1 Softly whip the cream in a bowl, stir in the custard. Put in freezer for about 1½ hours, until it starts to freeze around the edge.
2 Meanwhile, put the sugar in a pan with 100ml/3½fl oz rum. Heat slowly to dissolve the sugar, tip in the fruits, and simmer gently for 1 minute. Pour into a wide bowl, and leave until cold (about an hour). Add the extra tablespoon of rum. Stir the cream and custard with a balloon whisk to break it all up, then stir in the cooled fruit. Pour into a 1.2-litre/ 2-pint pudding basin, cover and freeze overnight until firm (or for up to 1 month).
3 To serve, dip the basin quickly into boiling water, loosen the sides with a round-bladed knife, then turn the pudding out. Decorate with frosted bay leaves and grapes around the base.

• Per serving for 8 385 kcalories, protein 3g, carbohydrate 44g, fat 20g, saturated fat 13g, fibre 1g, added sugar 19g, salt 0.17g

This is inspired by trifle and tiramisu, taking some of the best elements of each. Top with a holly sprig for a festive touch.

Zabaglione Trifle Slice

FOR THE ZABAGLIONE CREAM
4 egg yolks
100g/4oz golden caster sugar
100ml/3½fl oz white wine, not too dry
100ml/3½fl oz marsala
284ml carton double cream

FOR THE PANETTONE AND FRUIT
225g/8oz panettone, sliced
3–4 tbsp marsala
425g can pitted black cherries, well drained

TO SERVE
cocoa powder, for sifting, and holly, to decorate

Takes 45 minutes, plus 45 minutes or overnight chilling • Serves 8

1 Whisk egg yolks and sugar for 2 minutes until falling in thick ribbons. Whisk in the wine, then marsala. Pour into a non-stick pan. Stir over a lowish heat 5–7 minutes until thickened and frothy. Pour into a bowl. Chill for 45 minutes (or overnight).
2 Line the base of a 20cm/8in round cake tin (5.5cm/2¼in deep) with overlapping slices of panettone. Drizzle over 3–4 tablespoons of marsala. Pat the cherries dry on kitchen paper, halve each one. Softly whip the cream, fold it into the cold marsala mix. If it's lumpy, beat with a wire whisk. Pour over the cherries. Open-freeze until firm, cover with cling film and foil. Freeze for up to 1 month.
3 To serve, unwrap and thaw in the fridge, about 2–2½ hours. Dust with cocoa powder.

• Per serving 417 kcalories, protein 4g, carbohydrate 36g, fat 27g, saturated fat 13g, fibre 1g, added sugar 20g, salt 0.18g

A ingenious dessert that looks impressive and tastes delicious served hot or cold.

No-Roll Mincemeat and Apple Tart

25g/1oz golden caster sugar
a generous pinch of cinnamon, nutmeg or mixed spice
225g circle ready-rolled shortcrust pastry, thawed of frozen
410g jar mincemeat
2 eating apples, peeled, cored and sliced

Takes 25 minutes • Serves 8

1 Preheat the oven to 220°C/Gas 7/fan oven 200°C. Mix the sugar and spice together in a small bowl. Unroll the pastry on to a flat baking sheet. Spoon the mincemeat in a rough circle over the middle of the pastry, scatter over the apple, then sprinkle with the spiced sugar.

2 Bring the pastry up around the edge of the filling, pressing the folds together with your fingers so that the sides stand up on their own.

3 Bake for 20 minutes until the pastry is golden and the apples have softened. Serve hot or warm with custard or ice cream.

• Per serving 293 kcalories, protein 2g, carbohydrate 52g, fat 10g, saturated fat 4g, fibre 2g, sugar 39g, salt 0.31g

The meringue will keep for a couple of weeks in a tin or in the freezer.

Pecan-toffee Meringue with Mulled Pears

FOR THE MULLED PEARS
6 small, ripe, shapely pears, peeled, quartered and cored
600ml/1pint mulled wine, ready-made from a bottle
50g/2oz golden caster sugar

FOR THE PECAN MERINGUE AND FILLING
1½ tsp cornflour
225g/8oz golden caster sugar
4 large egg whites
1½ tsp wine vinegar
50g/2oz pecans, roughly chopped
500g tub Greek yoghurt
4 tbsp dulce de leche
extra toasted pecans, for scattering

Takes 1 hour 40 minutes •
Serves 8–10

1 Simmer pears with the wine and sugar for 10 minutes. Preheat oven to 160°C/Gas 3/fan oven 140°C. Draw a 25cm/10in circle on a sheet of baking parchment. Put on a baking sheet. Mix cornflour and 225g/8oz sugar. Whisk egg whites until stiff. Whisk in sugar mixture, one spoon at a time, until thick and glossy. Fold in vinegar and half the nuts.
2 Pile mixture on to the circle, building up edges. Scatter with remaining pecans. Put in oven, lower temperature to 150°C/Gas 2/fan oven 130°C, bake for 1 hour. Turn oven off and cool inside for 1 hour.
3 Remove pears from juice, simmer juice until syrupy. Return pears and cool. Just before serving, mix yoghurt with dulce de leche. Pile the filling into the meringue and arrange pears on top. Scatter with nuts, serve with syrup.

• Per serving for 8 375 kcalories, protein 7.1g, carbohydrate 57.7g, fat 11.9g, saturated fat 4g, fibre 2.9g, sugar 56.4g, salt 0.24g

Packed with plump fruits with a whiff of rum, these are lighter than the traditional pudding. For children, replace rum with orange juice.

Mini Iced Christmas Puddings

finely grated zest 1 clementine
and 3 tbsp juice
5 tbsp golden rum
140g/5oz golden caster sugar
85g/3oz mix dried cranberries
and raisins
25g/1oz cut mixed peel
2 × 150g cartons light Greek
yoghurt
142ml carton double cream
50g/2oz white chocolate, melted
and piped in star shapes

Takes 30–35 minutes, plus cooling
and freezing • Serves 4

1 Line four 200ml/7fl oz moulds with cling film, leave an overhang. Heat the clementine juice with the rum and sugar until it dissolves. Tip in the dried fruit, simmer 2 minutes. Stir in the mixed peel and zest, leave until cold.
2 Beat the yoghurt with a spoon until smooth. Softly whip the cream, fold into the yoghurt. Measure off 4 tablespoons of the fruit and its syrup, set aside (or freeze). Stir the rest into the yoghurt mixture. Spoon into the pudding moulds. Cover with the cling film, then foil. Freeze (for up to a month).
3 Thaw the puddings in the fridge for 1 hour. Tip them out, remove the lining, serve with the thawed fruit and syrup and a chocolate star.

• Per serving 494 kcalories, protein 6g, carbohydrate 60g, fat 23g, saturated fat 13g, fibre 1g, added sugar 39g, salt 0.22g

This dessert can be frozen, well wrapped, for up to 6 weeks.
Thaw in the fridge for 8 hours before serving.

Tia Maria Cheesecake

85g/3oz hot melted butter, plus extra butter for greasing
14 plain chocolate digestives, finely crushed
3 × 300g packs full-fat Philadelphia cheese, at room temperature
225g/8oz golden caster sugar
4 tbsp plain flour
2 tsp vanilla extract
2 tbsp Tia Maria
3 eggs
285ml carton soured cream

FOR THE TOPPING
142ml carton soured cream
2 tbsp Tia Maria
cocoa powder, for dusting
8 Ferrero Rocher chocolates, unwrapped

Takes 1 hour 5 minutes, plus cooling •
Serves 16

1 Preheat the oven to 180°C/Gas 4/fan oven 160°C. Line a 25cm/10in springform tin. Blend butter and biscuit crumbs. Press into the tin, bake for 10 minutes, cool.
2 Increase oven to 240°C/Gas 9/fan oven 220°C. Beat the cheese and sugar with an electric whisk until smooth. Whisk in the flour, vanilla, 2 tablespoons Tia Maria, eggs and soured cream.
3 Butter sides of tin. Pour in mixture and smooth. Bake 10 minutes, then lower oven to 110°C/Gas ¼/fan oven 90°C, bake for 25 minutes. Turn oven off, open the door and leave to cool inside for 2 hours.
4 Mix soured cream and Tia Maria, smooth over cheesecake. Chill. Transfer to a plate. Dust top with cocoa. Mark the cheesecake into portions, decorate with chocolates.

• Per serving 410 kcalories, protein 7g, carbohydrate 32g, fat 29g, saturated fat 17g, fibre 1g, sugar 24g, salt 0.89g

Turn a sweet, scented dessert wine into a pretty,
shimmering jelly.

Beaumes-de-Venise Jelly

700ml/1¼ pint Muscat de
Beaumes de Venise or other
sweet dessert wine
gelatine powder or leaf gelatine
(see note in method)
50g/2oz caster sugar

Takes 15 minutes, plus 3–4 hours to
set • Serves 6

1 Pour half the wine into a small pan, sprinkle over the powdered gelatine or crumble in the leaves and allow to soak for a few minutes until spongy. Stir in the sugar.

2 Heat the mixture without allowing it to boil, stirring until the gelatine has dissolved completely. Remove from the heat, stir in the rest of the wine. Cool.

3 Pour the cool, but still liquid, jelly into a wetted, 700ml/1¼ pint mould or individual glasses and chill until firm.

Note: If serving in glasses use 1 tablespoon of powdered gelatine or 3 gelatine leaves for a soft set, but if you want to set it in a mould and turn it out, use 5 teaspoons of powdered gelatine or 5 leaf gelatine.

• Per serving 151 kcalories, protein 2g, carbohydrate 16g, fat none, saturated none, fibre none, added sugar 9g, salt 0.04g

A zingy and fresh-tasting dessert that provides
the perfect antidote to the Christmas excesses.

Caramelized Oranges
with Grand Marnier

4 oranges
4 tbsp Grand Marnier
25g/1oz shelled pistachios or flaked
almonds, toasted, coarsely
chopped
50g/2oz caster sugar
crème fraîche, to serve

Takes 25 minutes • Serves 4 (easily
doubled)

1 With a zester take all the rind off one of the
oranges, making small ribbons, and reserve.
Peel all the oranges, discarding the pith, then
cut them in half horizontally.
2 Put them into an ovenproof serving dish
and pour the Grand Marnier on top. Scatter
over some of the pistachios or almonds.
3 Add the sugar to 2 tablespoons of water in
a small heavy-based pan. Heat gently. When
the sugar starts browning and has a rich,
golden caramel colour, add the rind.
Stir the mixture together briefly then pour
immediately on to the orange halves.
Do not toss. Serve lightly chilled, scattered
with remaining nuts, and with spoonfuls of
crème fraîche.

• Per serving 177 kcalories, protein 3g, carbohydrate
27g, fat 4g, saturated fat 0g, fibre 3g, added sugar
13g, salt 0.02g

This is loosely based on the Scottish classic, Cranachan,
a blend of toasted oatmeal, raspberries, whisky and cream.

Iced Raspberry Cranachan Trifle

225g/8oz clear honey or
golden syrup
175ml/6fl oz whisky
225g/8oz fresh or frozen raspberries
(thawed if frozen), plus 100g/4oz
to decorate
50g/2oz oat-based muesli
100g/4oz golden caster sugar
500ml tub raspberry sorbet
850ml/1½ pints double cream
8 egg yolks

Takes 1½ –1¾ hours, plus overnight
freezing • Serves 8

1 Warm 4 tablespoons of honey with 6 tablespoons of whisky. Spoon raspberries into a freezer-proof serving bowl, pour honey mix over, stir, cool. Heat muesli and sugar in a small pan until it caramelizes. Pour on to a lightly oiled baking sheet. When cold, break into rough pieces and whiz half in a food processor to chop finely. Store rest.
2 When raspberries are cold, scoop sorbet on top. Lightly whip 600ml/1 pint of the cream, slowly adding whisky. Warm remaining honey in a pan. Whisk egg yolks for 4–5 minutes, adding the hot honey until lightly thickened. Fold in whipped cream and muesli. Spoon on to sorbet, freeze overnight.
3 Whip remaining cream, spoon over, top with muesli and raspberries. Leave at room temperature 10 minutes before serving.

• Per serving 864 kcalories, protein 7g, carbohydrate 63g, fat 61g, saturated fat 36g, fibre 1g, sugar 54g, salt 0.24g

These sundaes are the ultimate in elegance for a festive dinner party and can be made and chilled up to 2 hours in advance.

Cranberry and Pear Christmas Sundaes

2 large pears, Conference or Comice, cored, peeled cut into 12 wedges
600ml/1 pint cranberry juice
1 tbsp golden caster sugar
75g pack dried cranberries
4 tbsp ruby port or sweet sherry
1 sachet (11.7g) powdered gelatine, dissolved in 4 tbsp water
5–6 trifle sponges, broken into pieces
50g/2oz white chocolate, broken into pieces
284ml carton double cream
chopped unsalted fresh pistachios or toasted hazelnuts, for sprinkling

Takes 1–1¼ hours, plus 1–1½ hours chilling • Serves 6

1 Put the pears in a pan with the cranberry juice, sugar and cranberries. Bring to the boil, simmer for about 3–5 minutes until softened. Add the port and cook for 2 minutes. Strain into a heatproof jug, cool for 10 minutes, then whisk in the gelatine. Cool completely.
2 Divide sponges among six glasses. Put a pear wedge in each, spoon over half the cranberries. Pour over cranberry juice, press on the sponge. Chill until set, 1–1½ hours.
3 Meanwhile, melt the chocolate with 2 tablespoons of cream. Cool until tepid. Whisk the remaining cream with the tepid chocolate to soft peaks. Spoon into glasses. Chill until needed. To serve, decorate with remaining pear wedges (each halved lengthways) and cranberries, and a sprinkling of nuts.

• Per serving 504 kcalories, protein 5g, carbohydrate 53g, fat 30.5g, saturated fat 16.2g, fibre 2.1g, sugar 47g, salt 0.14g

Ideal for when there are just the two of you
to celebrate Christmas.

Sticky Cinnamon Figs

4 ripe figs
a knob of butter
2 tbsp clear honey
2–3 tbsp Armagnac or brandy
a small handful of shelled pistachio
nuts or almonds
½ tsp ground cinnamon or mixed
spice
mascarpone or thick Greek yoghurt,
to serve

Takes 10 minutes • Serves 2

1 Preheat the grill to medium-high. Cut a deep cross in the top of each fig, then ease the top apart so it opens like a flower.
2 Sit the figs in a small baking dish and drop a piece of butter into the centre of each frut. Drizzle the honey over the figs, then the Armagnac or brandy. Scatter over the nuts and spice.
3 Grill for 5 minutes until the figs are softened and the honey and butter make a sticky sauce in the bottom of the dish. Serve warm with dollops of mascarpone or yoghurt.

• Per serving 186 kcalories, protein 3.6g, carbohydrate 24.1g, fat 9.1g, saturated fat 2.8g, fibre 1.7g, added sugar 11.5g, salt 0.08g

With its rich mousse-like texture and indulgent cream filling,
this is the ultimate Swiss roll.

Christmas Chocolate Roulade

FOR THE ROULADE
175g/6oz dark chocolate, broken
into pieces
5 eggs, separated
175g/6oz caster sugar

FOR THE FILLING
2 tbsp Irish cream liqueur
284ml carton double cream, softly
whisked

FOR THE DECORATION
50g/2oz dark chocolate, melted
8 holly leaves, washed and dried,
brushed with melted chocolate,
leaves removed when set (or
use chocolate curls)
icing sugar, for dusting

Takes 40 minutes, plus cooling •
Serves 8

1 Preheat the oven to 180°C/Gas 4/fan oven 160°C. Line a 33×23cm/13×9in Swiss roll tin with baking parchment. Melt the chocolate for the roulade.

2 Whisk egg yolks and sugar in a bowl over a pan of simmering water, until the mixture leaves a trail when blades are lifted. Whisk in chocolate. Whisk egg whites to stiff peaks. Whisk a large spoonful into the chocolate mix, fold in the rest. Pour mixture into the tin, gently spread into the corners. Bake 20 minutes until firm. Cover loosely with foil, cool in tin for about 3 hours.

3 Stir liqueur into cream. Turn out roulade on to greaseproof paper. Spread with cream. Roll up from a short side. Decorate with icing sugar and chocolate leaves or curls.

• Per serving 429 kcalories, protein 6g, carbohydrate 40g, fat 28g, saturated fat 16g, fibre 1g, added sugar 38g, salt 0.16g

This dessert can be frozen up to a month ahead
then half-thawed before serving.

Mango and Passion Fruit Pavlova Roulade

FOR THE MERINGUE
2 tsp cornflour
2 tsp instant coffee powder
2 tsp white wine or cider vinegar
5 egg whites
225g/8oz golden caster sugar
a small handful of pistachios, sliced lengthways
icing sugar, for dusting

FOR THE FILLING
250g carton mascarpone, beaten
1 small mango, peeled and finely chopped
148ml carton double cream, whipped
1 passion fruit, halved, flesh scooped out

Takes 1 hour–1 hour 10 minutes, plus 30 minutes cooling • Serves 8

1 Preheat the oven to 140°C/Gas1/fan oven 120°C. Line a 33×23cm/13×9in Swiss roll tin with baking parchment. Mix cornflour, coffee and vinegar. Set aside. Whisk egg whites to stiff peaks, gradually beat in sugar until quite thick. Whisk in coffee mix. Spread onto the paper. Scatter over the pistachios. Bake for 35–40 minutes until it feels crisp.
2 Make filling. Mix mascarpone and mango, fold in the cream. Set aside.
3 Leave cooked meringue in tin for 10 minutes, then transfer to a cooling rack, paper-side down. When cold, tip out onto a sheet of baking parchment dusted with icing sugar, paper-side up. Discard lining paper, spread cream over meringue. Drizzle passion fruit over, roll up guided by sugared paper. Serve half-thawed, dusted with icing sugar.

• Per serving 378 kcalories, protein 4g, carbohydrate 34g, fat 26g, saturated fat 15g, fibre 1g, added sugar 26g, salt 0.21g

Index

Picture credits and recipe credits

BBC Worldwide would like to thank the following for providing photographs. While every effort has been made to trace and acknowledge all photographers, we would like to apologize should there be any errors or omissions.

Marie-Louise Avery p23, p39, p41, p49, p53, p67, p99, p107, p109, p111, p179; Martin Brigdale p187; Peter Cassidy p137, p183, p185, p189, p195, p211; Jean Cazals p69, p141, p151, p193, p197, p209; Ken Field p143, p167; Charlie Gray p105, p113, p149; Will Heap p207; David Munns p35, p65, p153, p169, p171, p173, p205; Noel Murphy p81, p83; Lis Parsons p37, p85, p87, p177; Craig Robertson p95, p191; Simon Smith p27; Roger Stowell p19, p31, p71, p75, p77, p79, p97, p129, p133, p135, p145, p161, p199, p203; Martin Thompson p43, p73, p101, p163; Debi Treloar p159; Simon Walton p89, p115, p125; Philip Webb p11, p13, p15, p21, p29, p33, p47, p55, p57, p59, p61, p63, p93, p117, p119, p121, p123, p127, p131, p139, p165, p175, p201; Simon Wheeler p147, p155, p181; Geoff Wilkinson p17, p25, p45, p91, p103; Peter Williams p157; Elizabeth Zeschin p51

All the recipes in this book have been created by the editorial team on *BBC Good Food Magazine*:

Lorna Brash, Sara Buenfeld, Mary Cadogan, Barney Desmazery, Jane Hornby, Emma Lewis, Kate Moseley, Orlando Murrin, Vicky